OUTDOOR LIFE

DISASTER SURVIVAL GUIDE

TOP SKILLS FOR DISASTER PREP

OUTDOOR LIFE

DISASTER SURVIVAL GUIDE

TOP SKILLS FOR DISASTER PREP

RICH JOHNSON
WITH ROBERT F. JAMES

weldon

CONTENTS

Intro by Rich Johnson
Survival Strategies
1 Create an At-Home Survival Kit
2 Stock an Office BOB
3 Gear Up with a To-Go BOB
4 Stop Bleeding
5 Disinfect a Wound
6 Build a First-Aid Kit
7 Bandage a Wound
8 Deal with Blood Loss
9 Immobilize an Arm Injury
10 Make a Splint
11 Set a Bone
12 Save with CPR
13 Perform the Heimlich Maneuver
14 Fake a Sling
15 Identify and Treat Burns
16 Treat for Shock
17 Be Ready for Disaster
18 Spot Tornado Warning Signs
19 Judge Where a Tornado Is Heading
20 Stay Safe in a Tornado
21 Reinforce Garage Doors in a Windstorm
22 Tree-Proof Your Home
23 Buck a Downed Tree
24 Make Waterproof Matches
25 Prepare Your House for a Hurricane
26 Build a Dike
27 Make DIY Flood Protection
28 Deal with a Downed Power Line in a Car
29 Survive a Severe Hurricane
30 Make a Life Raft from Household Items
31 Turn Your Attic into an Ark
32 Paddle Through Floodwaters
33 Drive Safely on Flooded Roads
34 Dig Your Truck Out of the Mud
35 Live Through a Flash Flood
36 Rescue Someone from a Flood
37 Return Home Safely After a Flood
38 Live Through Lightning
39 Help Someone Struck by Lightning
40 Install Lightning Rods
41 Protect Your Home from Wildfires
42 Prevent a Forest Fire
43 Survive a Wildfire
44 Withstand a Firestorm
45 Survive a Volcanic Eruption
46 Cope with Ash
47 Assess a Lava Field
48 Retrofit Your House
49 Keep Household Items Steady in a Quake
50 Know Earthquake Hot Spots
51 Understand Fault Activity
52 Ride Out a Quake in a Car
53 Survive Being Trapped Under Debris
54 Weather an Earthquake

55 Take Action After an Earthquake

56 Know Tsunami Warning Signs

57 Brace for a Big Wave

58 Deal with a Tsunami at Sea

59 Survive a Tsunami

60 Know When Mud Might Flow

61 Make It Through a Mudslide

62 Save Your Home from Mudslides

63 Know You're in Avalanche Country

64 Assess Incline

65 Recognize Avalanche Types

66 Ride Out an Avalanche

67 Know Which Way Is Up

68 Get Rescued from an Avalanche

69 Strap on a Safety Beacon

70 Walk in a Whiteout

71 Drive in a Blizzard

72 Survive in a Snowbound Car

73 Ride Out a Blizzard at Home

74 Store Food During a Blizzard

75 Prevent Carbon Monoxide Poisoning

76 Clear Heavy Snow

77 Cover Your Face in a Sandstorm

78 Drive in a Sandstorm

79 Pick a Safe Seat on a Train

80 Stop a Train

81 Get Your Car Off the Tracks

82 Jump from a Moving Train

83 Use Your Cell for an Airborne SOS

84 Contact Air Traffic Control

85 Jump Out of an Airplane

86 Salvage a Crash Site

87 Make It to the Lifeboat

88 Abandon Ship Safely

89 Swim Through Burning Oil

90 Handle a Hazmat Situation

91 Decontaminate Yourself

92 Seal Your Home from a Toxic Spill

93 Get Clear of a Hazard

94 Don a Gas Mask

95 Prevent the Spread of Illness

96 Dispose of a Body

97 Bunk Up in a Bunker

98 Anticipate Radiation's Effects

99 Get Through a Power Outage

100 Survive a Heat Wave

101 Eat Right in a Blackout

102 Start Your Car with a Screwdriver

103 Siphon Fuel

104 Charge Your Phone with a Flashlight

105 Harness a Car Battery

Index

About the Author

Credits and Acknowledgments

Dear Reader,

Great news! You're reading this book, and that means you must be alive. Which means you're following my **NUMBER ONE RULE** for survival: Stay alive. So far, so good. I can tell you're going to be a good student.

RULE NUMBER TWO Attitude trumps everything else. If your brain's not in the game, the rest of you will suffer for it. Survival is mental—and I'm not talking about your education, I'm talking about your mindset. As important as it is to know proper survival techniques, if your attitude stinks, you're probably not going to make it. Eliminate the word "quit" from your vocabulary. QUIT is a four-letter word, and around here we don't talk like that (unless a bear is gnawing on us).

RULE NUMBER THREE Don't take avoidable risks. Always look for the safest path, and pace yourself to prevent injuries. Do the things you want to do—but be smart about how you do them.

RULE NUMBER FOUR Live with integrity—and a big part of that is caring about others. Find ways to help people through rough spots. Lift those who need lifting; someday you'll need lifting, too.

RULE NUMBER FIVE Continually work to better your situation, especially if it's dodgy. Even small improvements to comfort or security will improve your spirits. And possibly save your bacon.

MY PHILOSOPHY IN A NUTSHELL To give yourself the best chance for survival, fill your head with accurate information, fill your hands with skill, and fill your life with experience. Let wisdom be your guide and common sense your pattern.

Take care out there,

Rich John

➕ SURVIVAL STRATEGIES

KNOW WHAT'S HAPPENING Problems can arise when you're not paying attention. If you remain cognizant of your surroundings, then you can respond appropriately.

PRIORITIZE Once you know what kind of fix you're in, decide what your most pressing need is. If your buddy has a bullet in his leg, your most pressing need isn't hunting dinner.

DEVISE A PLAN Now that you know what needs to be done first (and next, and then next), decide how to attack the problem. Weigh your options, then make smart decisions that will give you the desired result.

GO TO WORK The time has come for the rubber to meet the road. As you work on resolving each challenge, continually assess the situation. Decide if what you're doing is working, or if you need to change strategies.

Remember, you're trying to survive, and that's a worthy goal if ever there was one. Give it your all and good luck!

001

CHECKLIST
Create an At-Home Survival Kit

Outdoor adventurers know not to venture into the wild without the necessary survival gear. But what about when you're at home? Or out running errands? No matter where you are, you should always have certain survival essentials at hand. And while there's no such thing as a universal "bug-out bag" (called a "BOB" for short), you can assemble a variety of kits for every situation.

Start off by putting together the items below to create a fully stocked at-home kit that can meet the needs of you and your family in a disaster scenario. Store it someplace accessible so that you're always at the ready.

- ☐ Nonperishable food (a three-day supply for each person)
- ☐ Small stove with propane or other fuel
- ☐ Kitchen accessories and cooking utensils
- ☐ Can opener
- ☐ Three-day supply of water (1 gallon/3.75 l per person, per day)
- ☐ Water-purification tablets
- ☐ Bleach (add to water to make a mild disinfectant, or use 16 drops per gallon/3.75 l to purify water)
- ☐ Portable, battery-powered radio or television and extra batteries
- ☐ Flashlight and extra batteries
- ☐ Battery-operated, hand-cranked, or solar-powered cell-phone charger
- ☐ Tools, such as a wrench used for shutting off utilities, a screwdriver, and a hammer
- ☐ First-aid kit and manual
- ☐ Sanitation and hygiene items, such as soap, moist towelettes, toilet paper, and towels
- ☐ Items for infants, such as formula, diapers, bottles, and pacifiers
- ☐ Signal mirror and whistle
- ☐ Extra clothing for each person, including a jacket, coat, long pants, and long-sleeved shirt
- ☐ Hat, mittens, scarf, or other climate-specific clothing for each person
- ☐ Sturdy hiking or athletic shoes and socks
- ☐ Sleeping bag or warm blanket for each person
- ☐ Special-needs items, such as prescription medications, eyeglasses, contact-lens solution, and hearing-aid batteries
- ☐ Photocopies of passports, credit and identification cards
- ☐ Coinage and paper money in small denominations
- ☐ Plastic bags in various sizes
- ☐ Ground cloth or tarp
- ☐ Powdered, chlorinated lime to treat waste and discourage insects
- ☐ Strike-anywhere matches in a waterproof container

002 Stock an Office BOB

Disaster can strike at any time, including when you're at work. That's why it's smart to keep a BOB in your office or under your desk. It should include a set of rugged clothes (because scaling a wall in a suit is rarely a good idea), athletic shoes and socks (have you ever tried running in heels?), and a few food items and bottles of water. Toss everything in a single grab-and-go tote so you can evacuate efficiently, and then stash it in a drawer and forget about it. You'll be thankful to have it should your work environment ever become truly unpleasant.

003 CHECKLIST
Gear Up with a To-Go BOB

If you have to grab one bag and run because the world is caving in, that bag had better contain what you need for short-term survival. And since most of us evacuate in our cars, it's a good idea to keep this bag in your trunk, along with crucial road-safety items.

- ☐ Energy bars, trail mix, and a couple of separately packaged, ready-to-eat meals
- ☐ Several bottles of water, a filter, and water-purification tablets
- ☐ Tent and sleeping bag
- ☐ Fire striker and basic lighter, plus tinder cubes
- ☐ One entire change of clothing (such as pants, shirt, socks, underwear, gloves, hat, windbreaker, and poncho)
- ☐ Flashlight and extra batteries
- ☐ Knife and spork

- ☐ Military-grade can opener
- ☐ Heavy cord, snare wire, and fishing lures
- ☐ Battery-operated radio
- ☐ Battery-operated, hand-cranked, or solar-powered cell-phone charger
- ☐ First-aid kit and manual
- ☐ Sanitation and hygiene items, such as toilet paper, soap, and a small towel
- ☐ Special-needs items, such as medications, eyeglasses, contact-lens solutions, and hearing-aid batteries
- ☐ Signal mirror and whistle

- ☐ Any car-safety items, such as a spare tire, a tire iron, jumper cables, a windshield scraper, and hazard flares, plus any needed winter items (a small collapsible shovel, tire chains, and a bag of kitty litter)

004 STEP-BY-STEP
Stop Bleeding

No one likes to see blood coming out of somebody's body—least of all his or her own. But don't just cover it up: It's pressure that stops the bleeding. Here's how you can squeeze off the flow.

STEP ONE Locate the source of the bleeding. Got multiple cuts? Then deal with the worst one first.

STEP TWO Place a sterile compress directly over the wound and apply firm pressure. Don't be afraid to push hard. If the cut is on an extremity, place pressure on both sides of the limb so that it doesn't bend back and away from the pressure.

STEP THREE If the compress soaks through, don't remove it. Simply add another compress on top of the first and continue with the pressure. Keep stacking bandages until the bleeding has stopped.

STEP FOUR Remove the compresses and flush the wound with water to clean.

005 STEP-BY-STEP
Disinfect a Wound

Knowing how to disinfect a wound can be critical. Even small cuts can become infected—especially when you're out in the wilderness, which is not renowned for its sterility. And when your body is fighting off an infection, it's diverting valuable resources away from your overall health, leaving you susceptible to other illnesses and complications.

STEP ONE Stop the bleeding and assess the injury. If the bleeding won't stop, or if the wound is deep and you can tell it'll need stitches, seek medical attention. If you're going to the hospital, don't bother with cleaning a severe wound. Leave it to a pro.

STEP TWO Flush the wound with clean water. There's no need to use hydrogen peroxide, as the burning sensation doesn't mean the wound is getting cleaner—it 's actually causing tissue damage.

STEP THREE Thoroughly saturate the wound with a triple antibiotic ointment before applying a dressing in order to keep out dirt and debris.

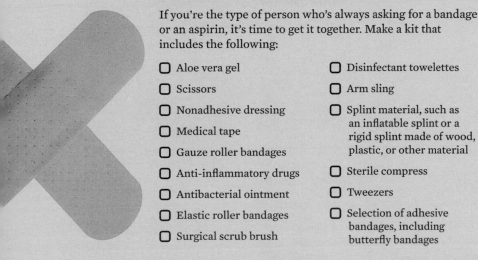

006
CHECKLIST
Build a First-Aid Kit

If you're the type of person who's always asking for a bandage or an aspirin, it's time to get it together. Make a kit that includes the following:

- ☐ Aloe vera gel
- ☐ Scissors
- ☐ Nonadhesive dressing
- ☐ Medical tape
- ☐ Gauze roller bandages
- ☐ Anti-inflammatory drugs
- ☐ Antibacterial ointment
- ☐ Elastic roller bandages
- ☐ Surgical scrub brush

- ☐ Disinfectant towelettes
- ☐ Arm sling
- ☐ Splint material, such as an inflatable splint or a rigid splint made of wood, plastic, or other material
- ☐ Sterile compress
- ☐ Tweezers
- ☐ Selection of adhesive bandages, including butterfly bandages

007

Bandage a Wound

It takes 72 hours for skin to close up and become airtight. For small cuts and scrapes, just keep the area clean. For large cuts, you may need to do a bit more to take care of the injury.

DON'T STITCH IT UP We've all seen our action heroes use a needle and thread. Unless you have sterile sutures, a suture needle, and a tool to get the hook through the skin, this option isn't happening. (Likewise, leave sterilizing and closing a wound with a hot knife blade to the stars on the big screen.)

BUTTERFLY IT The best way to close a wound is to apply sterile adhesive strips after disinfecting it. First, line up the edges of the cut. Then, starting in the center of the wound, place an adhesive strip's end on one side of the cut. As you lay the strip across the wound, push the wound's edges together. Apply these bandages in a crisscross pattern down the length of the cut to keep the sides in contact, then dress with a sterile wrap.

BE SUPER In a pinch, superglue can hold your skin closed—it worked for soldiers in the Vietnam War. Just make sure you coat only the outside edges of the cut, not in the cut itself.

008 ASSESS AND RESPOND
Deal with Blood Loss

When you're in the outdoors, many objects you encounter will be pointed, jagged, or razor-sharp. Your tender human flesh doesn't stand a chance against a misdirected axe or an errant blade, and that doesn't even begin to take into account accidents involving sharp rocks, or a skin-shredding tumble on a

 OOZE An abrasion or common scrape tears open capillaries, resulting in a slow trickle of blood from the wound. Infection is your biggest threat here.

- Disinfect the wound.

- Use moderate pressure to stop the bleeding.

- Keep the wound moist with aloe vera or antibiotic ointment until it heals.

- Cover it with a semipermeable dressing.

- Change the dressing daily and inspect the wound for infection, which might require professional treatment.

 SPURT If bright red blood shoots from the wound, you have arterial bleeding, and it's highly dangerous. Forget disinfecting; just stop the bleeding.

- Elevate the injury above the heart.

- Aggressively apply pressure.

- If a wound on a limb won't stop bleeding, tie a tourniquet above the wound and tighten it until the blood stops flowing. But be warned that the use of a tourniquet can lead to the necessity for amputation. Use one only when you must.

- Call 911 or transport the victim to the nearest available medical facility immediately.

trail. So it's little surprise that blood-loss injuries are the most common afflictions in outdoor situations. Since there's a whole world of possible damage you can do to yourself out there, here are four common categories of bleeding and what to do for each.

 FLOW If dark red blood gushes steadily, a vein has been opened. You've got to clean the wound and stop the flow until you can get the victim to a hospital.

- Elevate the injury above the heart.

- Use tweezers to remove any debris that is lodged in the cut. Disinfect the wound.

- Apply direct pressure to the injury. You can apply pressure with bare hands at first, but then search for something to serve as a direct-pressure pad.

- After the bleeding stops, use tape or cloth strips to secure the dressing over the wound.

 INTERNAL If someone has been in a high-speed automobile accident or if a sharp object hit near an organ, he or she may be bleeding on the inside.

- Monitor for hypovolemia (a state in which blood levels are drastically reduced). Shock, pallor, rapid breathing, confusion, and lack of urine are all signs.

- Incline the victim toward the injured side. This constrains the blood flow to the damaged area, and keeps the good side up and running.

- Stabilize the victim, treat for shock, and call 911 or transport the victim to a medical facility immediately.

009

STEP-BY-STEP
Immobilize an Arm Injury

Boy, it sure is useful to have two working arms. But if you've injured one (with a fracture, a severe sprain, or an especially gnarly cut), you'll need to immobilize it for a while. Fashioning a sling is pretty straightforward, but it's a core bit of knowledge to have at your disposal; in particular, use this method if you're out in the wild and away from medical care.

STEP ONE Start with a square cloth approximately 3 by 3 feet (1 m by 1 m). Lay the cloth out flat, then fold it once diagonally to make a triangle.

STEP TWO Slip the injured arm into the fold, and bring both ends up around the neck, slanting the forearm up slightly.

STEP THREE Tie the corners in a knot. Gravity will naturally pull the forearm back to parallel position.

STEP FOUR Use a belt to immobilize the arm against the body. Wrap it around the chest, above the forearm but away from the problematic zone. Cinch it closed but not too tightly, as maintaining circulation is key.

010 STEP-BY-STEP
Make a Splint

If someone injures a leg in the wild, immobilization is key—but you still have to walk back to civilization, so staying still isn't an option. So craft a splint with a sleeping pad, cardboard, or other flexible material.

STEP ONE Stop any bleeding with direct pressure.

STEP TWO Check for a pulse below the fracture and look at the skin—if it's pale, circulation may be cut off and you may need to set the bone (see item 11).

011 Set a Bone

If you've ever heard the grim sound of a bone breaking, you know just how dire this situation can be. Getting to a hospital is always the best recourse, but if you can't, setting the bone in place might be the only way to save the arm or leg. Here's how to do it.

ASSESS THE BREAK Many breaks don't need setting, but a few, such as transverse, oblique, or impacted fractures, might. If a bone is actually protruding from the skin, don't try to set it. Just immobilize it.

CHECK FOR BLOOD FLOW Press on the skin below the fracture site. The skin should turn white and then quickly return to pink. Pale or bluish skin, numbness, tingling, or the lack of a pulse in the limb indicate a loss of circulation, and you will need to set the bone to restore circulation.

PUT IT IN PLACE To reduce swelling, pain, and damage to tissues caused by lack of circulation, realign the limb into a normal resting position by pulling in opposite directions on both sides of the break.

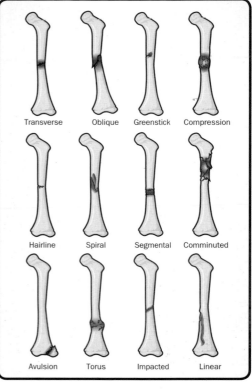

Transverse   Oblique   Greenstick   Compression

Hairline   Spiral   Segmental   Comminuted

Avulsion   Torus   Impacted   Linear

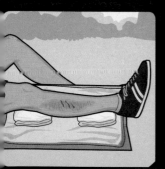

STEP THREE
Slide the unfolded splint material beneath the limb, and pad it for comfort and stability.

STEP FOUR
Fold the splint around the leg, securing it with elastic, gauze, or other material. The splint should be just tight enough to prevent the bone from shifting, but not so tight that it impedes circulation. If the break involves a joint, secure the splint both above and below it for extra stability.

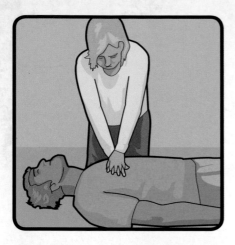

012

STEP-BY-STEP
Save with CPR

It's an absolute nightmare: Someone in your group loses his or her pulse and quits breathing, and it's up to you to get blood flowing to the heart and brain. The mere thought of this scenario should convince you to get trained in cardiopulmonary resuscitation (CPR). But if you're untrained, you can still help. Here's how.

STEP ONE Call 911. This is life or death, and you should get medics on the scene as soon as possible.

STEP TWO Place the heel of your hand on the middle of the victim's chest (just a couple of inches above the bottom of the sternum) and stack your other hand on top of the first.

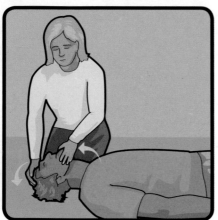

STEP THREE Begin compressions on the victim's chest, pushing 2 inches (5 cm) down. Keep your elbows locked, and for an adult victim, put your full weight over him or her—the more force, the better.

STEP FOUR Pump at a rate of 100 beats per minute, continuing until help arrives or the victim recovers. If other people are nearby, take turns performing compressions, as the effort will tire you easily.

STEP FIVE If you are certified in CPR, stop after 30 compressions and gently tip back the victim's head to open up his or her airway.

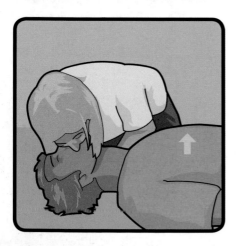

STEP SIX Again, only if you've been certified, pinch the victim's nose. Seal your mouth over his or hers, and give two deep breaths. Keep repeating the entire process until help arrives or the victim recovers.

013

Perform the Heimlich Maneuver

A choking victim can't tell you what's wrong or how to help him or her. Usually, people with a constricted airway will wrap their hands around their throat, but it's up to you to recognize the situation and act fast. Here's how to help if you're dealing with an adult who's choking.

STEP ONE Stand behind the victim and place one arm around the waist. Put your fist below the ribs but above the navel with your thumb turned toward the stomach.

STEP TWO Wrap your other arm around the victim's waist and cover your fist with the palm of this hand.

STEP THREE Press your fist into the abdomen with quick, upward thrusts. Don't press on the rib cage, and try to keep the force of the thrusts in your hands, not your arms.

STEP FOUR Repeat the thrusts until the object is dislodged and the victim's airway has been cleared.

If you can't reach around the victim's waist, or if the victim is unconscious, move the person to a supine position on the floor and perform the maneuver while straddling the victim's legs or hips.

014 Fake a Sling

No sling? No problem. When it comes to immobilizing an arm, just about any kind of cloth or material can work, so look around. For instance, you can place a loop of rope or a belt loosely around the neck, slide the arm inside so that the wrist rests in the loop, knot or cinch the rope or belt in place, and there you go: The arm is unlikely to bounce and incur further injury.

But let's say you're out on a hike without any rope, and—on today of all days— you're sporting pants with an elastic waistband. Try unbuttoning a few buttons in the center of your shirt and putting your hand through the hole, or placing your hand under the strap of your backpack. A pair of pants also makes for an easy tie—just use the crotch of your pants to support the arm, and knot the legs behind the neck. Sure, you may be the guy in the woods with your pants off, but if your arm's broken, you've got bigger problems to worry about.

015 Identify and Treat Burns

To comprehend burns and their severity, first you have to understand skin: It's the body's largest organ, and it's made up of three different layers of varying thicknesses. The severity of a burn depends on how deep into these layers it penetrates, and the treatment will likewise vary for each type of burn.

FIRST DEGREE Also known as superficial burns, these minor burns can be caused by anything from hot liquids to sun exposure. They heal on their own, but it's a good idea to remove any constraining jewelry or clothing and apply a cool compress or aloe vera gel. Anti-inflammatory drugs will hasten healing.

SECOND DEGREE Flame flashes, hot metals, and boiling liquids cause this burn, which usually penetrates the skin's second layer. You'll know if you've got one because blisters will form, and it takes longer than a few days to heal. Usually it's enough to flood the site with cool water and trim away any loose skin (but leave the blisters intact to prevent infection). A daily slather of aloe vera and a nonadhesive dressing are also recommended. The exception? If the burn is larger than 3 inches (7.5 cm) in diameter, or if the burn is on the victim's face, hands, feet, groin, or bottom, it's best to go to an emergency room for care.

THIRD DEGREE This full-thickness burn is very severe. It reaches through all three layers of the skin. In the event of a third-degree burn, treat the victim for shock and transport him or her to a hospital. Skin grafts are always required.

FOURTH DEGREE Another full-thickness burn, the fourth-degree burn damages structures below the skin, such as ligaments and tendons. These burns are bad news: They destroy nerves, so the victim won't feel anything. Amputation and permanent disability are likely, so your best bet is to evacuate the victim to a medical facility immediately.

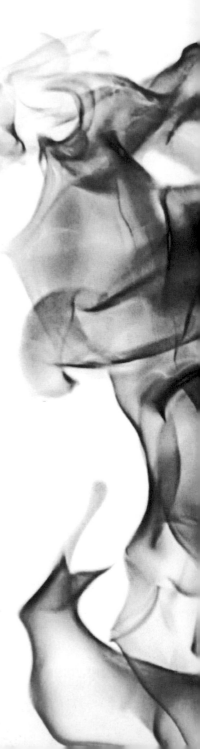

016 STEP-BY-STEP
Treat for Shock

During trauma, the circulatory system diverts the body's blood supply to vital internal organs. This redistribution of oxygen can ultimately lead to shock, which is fatal if not treated properly. Pain and fear both contribute to shock, compounding the danger from the injury.

STEP ONE Recognize the symptoms of shock, such as rapid pulse, gray or pale skin (especially around the lips), and cold, clammy skin on which the sweat doesn't evaporate. Other symptoms, such as gasping for air, nausea, and vomiting, can occur as the condition worsens.

STEP TWO Have the victim lie down, keeping his or her head low. Treat any outward injuries, such as bleeding.

STEP THREE Elevate the victim's feet slightly, carefully avoiding any injuries to the legs.

STEP FOUR Loosen restrictive clothing, such as belts—it'll help the victim breathe more freely.

STEP FIVE Keep the victim warm with blankets or coats.

STEP SIX Keep talking to focus the victim's mind, and reassure him or her that all will be well.

017 Be Ready for Disaster

A tidal wave washes hundreds of people out to sea in an instant. A hurricane doubles a region's homeless population overnight. A tornado knocks out a city's power grid. None of us is safe from nature's whims. But educating yourself on what to do in various situations can make a disaster less disastrous.

MAKE PLANS Know the kinds of trouble that are likely to arise in your area and think about how you and your family should respond to those situations. Pick out the spots that will be the safest refuge for each scenario, and make sure everyone knows emergency numbers, including the number of a trusted relative or friend who lives in another state.

HOLE UP AT HOME Your dwelling may be the safest place to ride out danger, so make sure it's always stocked with an at-home emergency kit. Have a bug-out bag packed in case you have to take off in a hurry, which you may well have to do.

PLOT YOUR ESCAPE When it comes to hurricanes and floods, your best chance may be to evacuate safely. As soon as there's a hint of trouble, start monitoring local reports and plan the safest, swiftest way out of the area to somewhere more secure.

RELY ON YOURSELF After a disaster, electricity and running water may be slow to return. Prepare yourself to live without them. It could save your life.

KNOW THE NUMBERS
Disasters

14,802 Deaths from the 2003 heat wave in France—more than any other European nation.

75 Percentage of Ukraine's wheat crop destroyed in the heat wave of 2003.

3.7 to 4 million People who died as a result of China's Great Flood of 1931.

1,720 feet (524 m) Tallest wave ever recorded, during Alaska's 1958 Lituya Bay mega tsunami.

11 million Gallons of crude oil spilled during the Exxon Valdez crisis on the Alaskan coast.

6.6 million Number of people exposed to dangerous levels of radiation from the Chernobyl power-plant accident.

RICH SAYS

"Disasters are like IRS audits: They strike when you least expect it, and they instantly turn your world upside-down. Preparation is key to survival."

RICH SAYS

"They call it a 'finger of God' for good reason. You'd best be on good terms with the man upstairs if you cross paths with a violent storm like this one."

Green Tinge

Wall Cloud

018 Spot Tornado Warning Signs

Is that shape on the horizon an innocent cloud—or a deadly tornado? As you scan the skies, keep an eye out for these telltale signs:

SUPERCELL Look for a thunderhead with a hard-edged, cauliflower look. This is a supercell: a dangerous cloud formation with interior winds of up to 170 miles per hour (273 km/h).

WALL CLOUD These have clearly defined edges and look dense and, well, sort of like a wall.

GREEN TINGE A sickly green hue in the sky can mean that a tornado is starting to take shape.

FUNNEL CLOUD A needle-shaped formation descending from a cloud's base indicates cyclonic activity. When a funnel cloud touches ground, it becomes a tornado. Fortunately, most funnel clouds never touch down.

STRANGE SOUNDS Listen for sounds similar to swarming bees or a waterfall—that may be an approaching twister you're hearing. If your ears pop, there's been a drop in air pressure, which is another danger sign.

019 Judge Where a Tornado Is Heading

If you're on the ground staring down a tornado, you can usually tell whether it's moving to your left or right. But if a tornado looks like it's standing still, you're right in its path—and you need to get out, quick.

Tornadoes often move southwest to northeast, so use a compass or a car's navigation system to avoid driving in the same direction. Of course, nothing beats the eyeball test. If you see a tornado, drive away at a right angle to its path. Don't try driving directly away from the twister—that'll put you exactly in the line of danger. There's an excellent chance that the tornado will overtake you, because twisters are difficult—sometimes downright impossible—to outrun.

020 ASSESS AND RESPOND
Stay Safe in a Tornado

A twister can touch down in the blink of an eye, so it's tough to know where you'll be or how bad the storm will get. Here's advice on staying safe in three likely situations, from a tornado that's hypothetical to one that's about to hit.

TORNADO THREAT Highly Possible

- Gather needed supplies.
- Clear shelter of hazards.
- Monitor broadcasts for details.
- Watch conditions for signs of supercell activities.
- Check in with friends and family members, and share plans and location information.

- Avoid back roads and unfamiliar places.
- Head for home or a designated shelter. If the weather becomes severe, pull over until it improves.
- Avoid using hazard lights, which may distract motorists.
- Monitor broadcasts.

TORNADO THREAT On the Ground

- Do not open doors or windows.
- Move to the basement or storm cellar if you have one, or to an interior room.
- Have a mattress or other padding ready to pull over your head.
- Prepare to move to a sturdier storm shelter if an evacuation warning is issued.

- Pull off the road and locate the tornado.
- If you can see a funnel, determine its direction.
- If you're in the tornado's path, drive immediately away at a right angle to its path.

TORNADO THREAT Coming Right at You

- Get into a bathtub or other fixture that's firmly adhered to the floor.
- Pull a mattress over your body to protect yourself from falling debris.
- Lock arms with others.
- Stay low and avoid the temptation to watch or film the tornado.

- Get out of the car.
- Find a low-lying area and lie flat with your fingers locked together behind your head.
- Do not go under an overpass, as the winds will increase there.
- If there's a large boulder, put your hands behind your head and crouch on the side that has some protection from the wind.

In a Shelter

 In a Car

 In the Open

- If you're camping, stay close to home base.
- Watch for tornadic signs in the southwestern sky.
- Stash your gear in your vehicle.
- Stay in groups.
- Contact a responsible person back home and fill him or her in on your situation and location.

- Stay out of tents or makeshift structures, which may collapse.
- Seek a low-lying area in which to ride out the storm.
- If you're in the tornado's path, move quickly to a ravine as far away from the path as possible.
- Keep low to avoid flying debris.

- Resist the temptation to watch what's going on. You need to focus on being a survivor, not a witness.
- Lie facedown with hands protecting your head in a low-lying area until the storm has passed.
- Look for a sturdy object like a boulder, and put it between you and the twister.

KNOW THE NUMBERS
Tornadoes

1,500 Number of tornadoes that occur annually worldwide.

1,200 Number of tornadoes that happen in the United States, thanks to a combination of geography (lots of low-lying flatland) and climatic conditions.

90 Percentage of U.S. tornadoes that occur in Tornado Alley, an area of the central United States.

80 Percentage of tornadoes in the United States that cause insignificant damage.

219 miles (352 km) Longest recorded damage track of a tornado.

7 feet (1.5 m) Shortest damage track.

300 miles per hour (482 km/h) Fastest wind speeds recorded in a tornado.

1 mile (1.6 km) Farthest a person has ever been flung by a tornado.

3 hours, 29 minutes Longest-lived tornado on record.

305 miles (491 km) The farthest confirmed distance an object was carried by a tornado. It was a cancelled check.

15 tons Weight of the heaviest item flung by a tornado: a piece of factory machinery.

021 Reinforce Garage Doors in a Windstorm

Battening down the hatches to prepare for a storm? Don't forget the garage. Double-wide garage doors are a weak spot in a windstorm, as high winds can cause these broad, flexible doors to bow inward and fall off their tracks. And that makes your garage, car, and home vulnerable to greater damage.

You could invest in a wind-resistant door, or reinforce the current door yourself with a kit that allows you to brace your door and still use it. But if a high-wind advisory has just been issued and you have to act fast, you can board up your garage door with wooden planks, just as you would your home's windows. Add horizontal and vertical bracing onto each panel of the door.

If you have an automatic garage-door opener, disable it to avoid accidental damage from someone trying to open the door while it's boarded up.

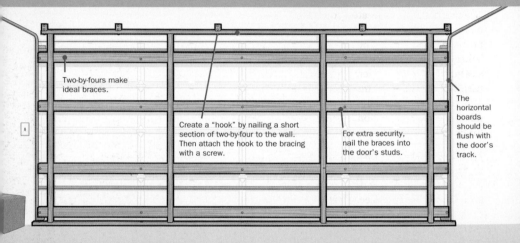

Two-by-fours make ideal braces.

Create a "hook" by nailing a short section of two-by-four to the wall. Then attach the hook to the bracing with a screw.

For extra security, nail the braces into the door's studs.

The horizontal boards should be flush with the door's track.

022 Tree-Proof Your Home

Large, mature trees can increase the value of your property—unless they crash into your house. Prune weak, damaged, or dead limbs, and consider these other steps to protect your home from tree damage.

CULL THE HERD The best way to tree-proof your home is to remove all trees from your yard that could reach your house if they were to fall.

PLANT DEFENSIVELY Remember that young saplings planted today will grow up to become big trees that might pose a danger to your house. So plant strategically, picking spots where trees won't threaten your home, your neighbor's house, and external features like power lines and propane tanks. Don't plant brittle species that are prone to breakage, such as elm, willow, box elder, poplar, and silver maple. Where ice storms are a possibility, don't plant trees that hold their leaves late into the fall. The weight of ice on leaves can bring down limbs or entire trees.

MAKE NICE WITH THE NEIGHBORS If the tree that's looming over your house belongs to your neighbors, use diplomacy to persuade them to remove the tree. That task will be easier if you can convince them that the tree is a danger to their own house as well.

023 STEP-BY-STEP Buck a Downed Tree

When severe weather hits, downed trees follow. Imitate a lumberjack and use the proper technique to cut up a tree on the ground—a process called "bucking."

STEP ONE Remove all major branches, then brace the underside of the tree with pieces of wood to keep the trunk stable and off the ground.

STEP TWO Standing uphill from the tree, start by cutting the underside of the trunk about one-third of the way through with a chainsaw. Then come back to the top side and finish the cut so it runs all the way through the trunk.

STEP THREE Gravity should pull that trunk section off the tree, but if your saw gets stuck in the cut, shut it off right away. Drive a wedge into the cut to loosen the tension, and then carefully remove the saw from the wood.

024

Make Waterproof Matches

When it comes to matches, the best ones are waterproof, especially in dire circumstances like a flood. Since they're much more expensive than their pedestrian cousins, you might want to make your own.

USE THE CANDLE TECHNIQUE
Burn a candle long enough for a pool of wax to form around the wick. Blow it out, then dip the head of your match into the wet wax, about ⅓ inch (3 mm) up the stick. Remove the matchstick and allow the wax to dry, pinching the wax closed to form a water-tight seal.

DEPLOY THE NAIL POLISH PLOY
Coat your matches with clear nail polish to waterproof them. Dip the head of the match and a bit of the matchstick itself into the polish, then rest the match on a counter with the head hanging off the edge to dry without sticking to anything.

TRY THE TURPENTINE TRICK
The easiest way to waterproof your matches is simply to drop them in turpentine. Allow the matches to soak for 5 minutes before placing them on newspaper to dry. After 20 minutes or so, you'll have a handful of waterproof matches that will last several months.

025

CHECKLIST
Prepare Your House for a Hurricane

If a hurricane is forecast, stay glued to weather reports, and if evacuation is advised, go. But if you have the all-clear to stick it out, ready yourself and your home.

☐ Stock up on nonperishable foods, prescriptions, and hygiene essentials.

☐ Cover windows with plywood. Use wood screws, not nails, anchored to the exterior walls.

☐ Lash down (or stow indoors) anything from your yard that might become a flying projectile in a storm.

☐ Assess which trees might be blown onto the house. Trim limbs that seem vulnerable, and avoid rooms under big trees once the storm starts.

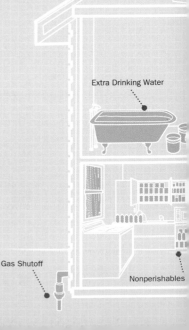

Extra Drinking Water

Gas Shutoff

Nonperishables

☐ Know how to turn off the gas, water, and electricity in case you're instructed or decide you need to do so.

☐ While the faucets are still flowing, fill up bathtubs, sinks, and buckets so you have an emergency supply if the water lines are cut off or contaminated by the storm.

☐ Shelter in an interior room away from windows. Take a radio—preferably a battery-operated or wind-up one—to keep up with news of the storm.

☐ For a fire-safety measure, set the bases of your emergency candles in a dish filled with water.

☐ Store valuables as high as possible—ideally in the attic. That's also a great place to stash an axe, which will prove useful if you need to break through to your roof to escape rising water.

☐ Don't be fooled into thinking the storm is over just because the weather becomes calm. Remain in shelter until after the eye passes, the storm renews its fury, and then gradually moves away.

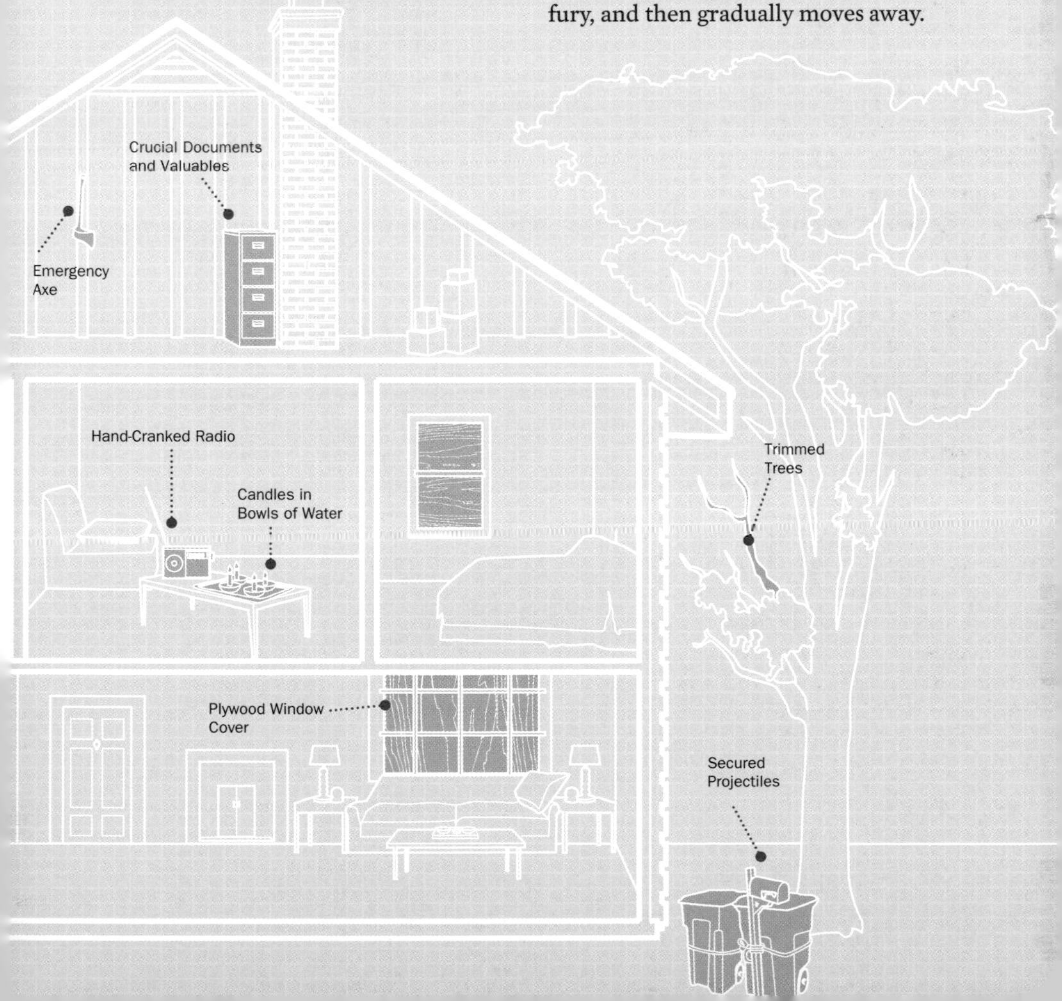

Crucial Documents and Valuables

Emergency Axe

Hand-Cranked Radio

Candles in Bowls of Water

Trimmed Trees

Plywood Window Cover

Secured Projectiles

026

Build a Dike

If floodwaters are threatening your home, use sandbags to create a dike.

PICK A SPOT Build the dike on the side of your yard from which water will be flowing. Don't erect the dike against a wall: The weight of these sandbags might compromise the building's structure.

FILL THE BAGS Put the first scoop of sand just inside the bag's mouth to hold it open, then fill it halfway full before tying off the top.

BUILD THE BARRIER Friction between sandbags and the ground holds the dike in place, so remove slippery substances like leaves. If you're going to build your dike more than 3 feet (1 m) high, increase its stability by placing the bottom row of bags in a shallow trench that's about 6 inches (15 cm) deep and 2 feet (61 cm) wide. Stagger the position of bags as you stack them, as if you were laying bricks. As a rule of thumb, the width of the dike at the bottom should be two or three times the overall height.

027

Make DIY Flood Protection

If you're caught without sandbags and an inundation is imminent, it's time to improvise. First off, be aware that you don't have to use sand to build your fortifications—dirt or small gravel will do in a pinch. Fill up pillowcases, tie off T-shirts and pants, or even use socks if need be. If you're building a fortification to protect your home, you can try piling up furniture as an armature, then filling in the gaps with your improvised sandbags. It doesn't have to be pretty; it just has to divert water.

028

Deal with a Downed Power Line in a Car

If a power line falls on your car and disables it while you're inside, you'll have to take action.

PUT OUT AN SOS The safest thing to do is remain in your vehicle and phone for help.

JUMP FREE If you must leave the vehicle because of fire or some other danger, avoid touching any metal portion of your car's frame. The greatest peril comes from touching the car and the ground at the same time, since electricity could travel through you into the ground, thus causing injury or death. Jump as far away from the car as you can, landing with feet together.

SHUFFLE OFF TO SAFETY Keep both feet in contact with each other and the ground as you move off. Avoid any pools of water, which conduct electricity.

029

CASE STUDY: WIND GONE WILD
Survive a Severe Hurricane

With Hurricane Katrina bearing down on his Gautier, Mississippi, home, Armand Charest decided to ignore the weather experts advising evacuation. Instead, he and his wife prepared to ride out the storm—much as they had ridden out previous hurricanes.

As the warnings grew more urgent, the Charests decided to take shelter with neighbors whose house was at a higher elevation. They brought along emergency food and water supplies to add to the essentials already at the home, such as a generator and extra gas in jerry cans. Once the power went out, they used a battery-powered TV to keep track of the storm's progress.

As the winds picked up and the storm surge began rising, the Charests and their hosts began rethinking their decision to stay. When the waters reached the tires of the vehicles parked in the front yard, they moved them across the street to the higher ground of a neighbor's driveway. The one remaining vehicle, which was left parked in the garage, was already floating in the floodwaters by the time they got back. Adding to their woes, the car's gas tank leaked, filling the house with fumes. To ventilate the house, they knocked out some of the plywood window covers and opened the windows wide. That, of course, exposed the interior of the house to the wind and rain of the storm.

Once the water level inside rose to their waists, Charest and his host swam out to a boat and tethered it to a column on the front porch in case they had to leave quickly. They spent the next several hours keeping dangerous floating debris, like propane tanks, away from the exterior of the house. As soon as the winds died down, they removed the remaining window reinforcements in an effort to better ventilate the house.

As the waters receded, Charest and his host managed to start one of the trucks across the street. They drove to Charest's home to discover it intact but flood damaged. He contacted family members farther north, who caravanned down to rescue the survivors. But their troubles still weren't over: They had to decide whether to cross a bridge that had been damaged when a crane broke from its moorings. They opted to take their chances and go over the bridge, which held up, luckily—a harrowing yet happy end to the ordeal.

POST ASSESSMENT
Wind Gone Wild

In August 2005, the Charest family and their friends chose to ride out Hurricane Katrina rather than evacuate. But as floodwaters continued to rise, they regretted their decision to stay behind.

 Prior to leaving his home, Armand Charest took precautions to make it hurricane resistant. He boarded up windows and exterior doors and covered all interior furnishings with plastic sheeting.

He put together disaster supplies to last through the chaos of the first 72 hours.

The Charests accepted an invitation to ride out the storm with friends whose house was at a higher elevation. Several other neighbors also were invited, providing safety in numbers.

As the floodwaters rose, they moved their cars to higher ground across the street.

They moored a boat to the porch in case they had to make a fast escape.

They worked to keep dangerous floating debris, like propane tanks, away from the house.

 Like so many others, Charest ignored warnings to evacuate as Hurricane Katrina approached.

He didn't prepare and place sandbags, which might have countered the storm surge.

Charest and his friend left a car parked in the garage, which spilled gas into the water and filled the house with fumes, forcing them to knock out the plywood protection they'd put on the windows.

The survivors chose to drive across a bridge even though a floating crane had damaged it. They made it—but their decision to trust infrastructure that was compromised could have given their survival story a tragic ending.

030

CHECKLIST
Make a Life Raft from Household Items

Home sweet home isn't so sweet when it's full of mucky water—especially when you are low on supplies and don't know if assistance is on the way. Since your furnishings aren't helping you much (who needs a hutch full of china plates if there's no food to eat off them?), get creative and turn one of them into a life raft. You can simply float away on one of these larger items, or secure several together with rope.

- ☐ Mattress
- ☐ Air compression tank
- ☐ Dining room table
- ☐ Lawn chair cushions
- ☐ Plastic trash cans
- ☐ Ice chest
- ☐ Children's float toys

- ☐ Plastic swimming pool
- ☐ Fiberglass bathtub
- ☐ Spare tire
- ☐ Large plastic tub
- ☐ Collection of smaller plastic jugs and bottles held together under a platform of boards

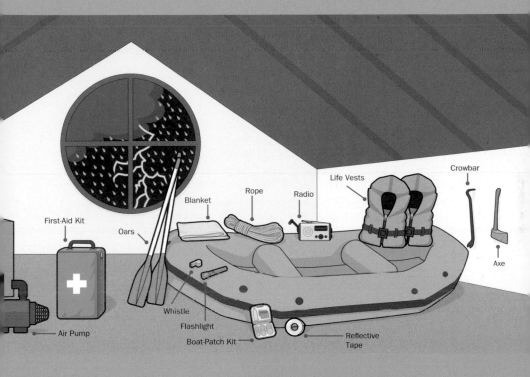

First-Aid Kit

Oars

Blanket

Rope

Radio

Life Vests

Crowbar

Axe

Air Pump

Whistle

Flashlight

Boat-Patch Kit

Reflective
Tape

031

Turn Your Attic into an Ark

You don't need to gather up a pair of every animal, but if you live in a flood zone, be prepared for rising waters. We've all seen scary images of homes flooded to their eaves, so learn from those lessons and keep your attic stocked as your getaway point. Equip an inflatable raft with vital supplies, including an air pump, flotation devices, a first-aid kit, and flares. Don't forget to include a patch kit for your raft.

If you have an exit point to the outside world through your attic, great. Otherwise, store an axe or a crowbar up there so you can break through the roof and escape if floodwaters keep rising.

032 Paddle Through Floodwaters

A canoe can be a great way to navigate or escape floodwaters. But there's a huge difference between fighting your way out of a hazard-filled flood zone and paddling down a lazy river.

SIT FOR STABILITY Place yourself slightly behind the middle of the boat with your weight low and centered.

TRY TO STAY DRY You know that floodwater is full of nasty stuff, so do your very best to stay out of it. No trailing your fingers in the water on this trip!

AVOID HIDDEN OBSTACLES Avoid swirls on the water's surface, since they may indicate a submerged object. In a big flood, you might encounter "overfalls," areas where water crosses a highway or other submerged feature. Overfalls often hide whirlpools and rapids, so steer away from them if you can.

PADDLE AWAY To steer the canoe through the current as straight as possible, stroke powerfully on alternating sides. Or use a strong J-stroke, turning and pushing the blade slightly outward at the end of the stroke to maintain better control of your speed and course.

033 Drive Safely on Flooded Roads

Every year, people lose their lives when their vehicles get washed away as they try to drive on flooded roads.

STUDY THE NUMBERS A measly 6 inches (15 cm) of water will cause most cars to lose control and possibly stall. Double that amount, and most cars just give up and float away. At 2 feet (60 cm) of rushing water, vehicles are at risk of being swept away (even trucks and four-wheel drives). If flood waters start swirling around your vehicle, abandon it—and save your life.

DON'T HEAD INTO THE UNKNOWN Beneath the water, pavement might be ripped away, leaving a hole that could swallow your vehicle. The rule for driving through water is simple: If you can't see the road surface or its line markings, take a detour.

034 Dig Your Truck Out of the Mud

Sure, getting your vehicle stuck in the mud can ruin your day. But when you're in a disaster (like, say, a major flood), and your escape mobile starts spinning its wheels in the dirt, this annoyance can escalate to a possibly deadly situation. Here's how to free your ride:

TAKE YOUR FOOT OFF THE GAS You don't want to dig deeper ruts and toss around the remaining solid ground under the wheels, so quit stomping on the gas pedal.

GO BACK AND FORTH Put the car in reverse and then drive forward; the wheels may pick up enough traction to move forward. Try it a few times.

KICK OUT YOUR PASSENGERS Have anyone in the car get out to lighten the load while you drive forward.

DIG A DITCH Using whatever tool you have on hand, hollow out a hole in the mud in front of each tire. Give each hole a slightly upward slope, then drive forward very gently and, with any luck, up the incline.

IMPROVISE GRIP Search your vehicle and the surrounding environment for branches, wooden planks, or blankets, and lay them immediately in front of the wheels. Then gently drive over these objects onto firmer ground.

035 Live Through a Flash Flood

You're exploring a canyon when, suddenly, the air rumbles like a subwoofer. Then you see it: a wall of water churning with felled trees and boulders. And it's headed your way.

KNOW THE AREA Avoid this hair-raising situation by staying away from flood-prone zones that are in the path of natural drainage areas such as riverbeds or canyons. If you're on the coast, beware of storm surges that may arise during tropical storms and hurricanes.

HIGHTAIL IT TO HIGH GROUND To escape a flash flood, you'll have to leave everything behind and run for high ground as fast as you can. If the water starts to rise around you, climb a tree or scramble onto a large rock—anything that will get you higher.

RIDE IT OUT If you end up in the flow, keep your head and upper body safe at all costs. Point your feet downstream and try to deflect—or better yet, steer clear of—obstructions like rocks and trees.

GET A GRIP You won't be able to fight the current, but you may be able to gradually work your way toward the edge of the flood so you can catch hold of a tree or bush and pull yourself out of the water.

HOLE UP AT HOME If a flash flood hits your house, arm yourself with essentials such as food, water, a battery-operated radio, and matches and candles and head for the upper floors. Unless your home's foundation is threatened and is on the verge of collapse, stay put until the waters recede.

036

STEP-BY-STEP
Rescue Someone from a Flood

The fast current of a flash flood is one of its biggest dangers. But if someone is trapped by a flash flood—clinging to a tree branch or perched on the roof of a car—try using that speed to your advantage.

STEP ONE Tie a rescue rope to a solid object (a tree, for example) to anchor it against the weight of the victim and the flowing water's immense pressure.

STEP TWO Coil the rescue rope and throw it upstream of the person you're rescuing, allowing the current to carry the line to the victim. Instruct that person to tie the rope around his or her waist.

STEP THREE Once secured to the rope, the victim can leave his or her perch and work toward the shore.

037 Return Home Safely After a Flood

After the all-clear sounds, you'll want to rush back home and assess the damage. But even once the waters recede, you may still be in danger. Follow these basic guidelines to stay safe.

CHECK OUT STRUCTURAL INTEGRITY If the foundation or roof looks damaged, have an inspector check out your home's stability before you go back inside.

AVOID OPEN FLAMES There may be gas leaks; After all you've been through, you probably don't want to deal with an explosion as well. So if the lights are out, don't light a candle.

HANDLE ELECTRICITY Turn off the power at the main circuit breaker or fuse box with something nonconductive, such as a broom or a rolled-up rubber mat. Wearing rubber gloves is also smart.

KEEP APPLIANCES OFF Have an electrician check out anything electrical or motorized that got wet.

DRAIN THE BASEMENT SLOWLY Emptying a flooded basement all at once can damage your home's stability. Drain a third of the water volume per day.

038 Live Through Lightning

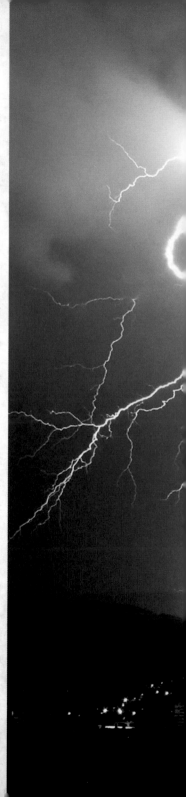

The shocking truth about lightning is that a discharge can travel 140,000 miles per hour (220,000 km/h), and the bolt's temperature can reach 54,000° F (30,000° C). Yikes! But if you're caught in a lightning storm, there are a few steps you can take to save your bacon—or, more accurately, to keep yourself from turning into bacon.

LISTEN FOR TROUBLE BREWING Sometimes lightning strikes without warning, but often there's a big, rumbling tip-off: the sound of thunder. As a storm approaches, thunder lags behind lightning about 5 seconds for each mile of distance. If you spot lightning, and thunder reaches you 10 seconds later, the strike was about 2 miles (3.2 km) away. That might sound reassuring, but it's not. A storm can move up to 8 miles (12.8 km) between strikes, so you're definitely in the danger zone.

SEEK SHELTER Safe shelters include substantial buildings and vehicles, which can act as a Faraday cage (a metallic enclosure that blocks electromagnetic fields). If you can't take shelter, at least head to low ground. Try to avoid water, open fields, and metal objects—especially tall ones like flagpoles. As for trees, standing by a lone tree is a no-no, but sheltering in a stand of trees will up your odds of survival.

SPREAD OUT There's usually safety in numbers—but not in this case. So spread out from your friends. As delightful as they are, they're also energy conductors.

LOSE THE BLING At the first signs of thunder and lightning, remove metal and jewelry from your body.

HEED THE FINAL WARNING If your hair stands on end or you hear crackling noises, place your feet together, duck your head, and crouch low with your hands on your knees.

GET LOW If you have one, put an insulating layer like a blanket on the ground, then crouch on it, keeping your hands off the ground to help the strike flow over your body rather than through it. This position is tough to maintain, so think of it as a last-resort move when a strike seems imminent.

039 Help Someone Struck by Lightning

Contrary to popular belief (and millions of cartoons), lightning victims usually aren't badly burned. You're more likely to be grappling with these symptoms:

A STOPPED HEART The primary cause of death in lightning-strike victims is cardiac arrest. It's also common for the strike to damage lungs, so a victim's breathing may stop as well. If you know how to perform CPR, chest compressions are the way to go.

PARALYSIS The victim may not be able to move or speak, due to an acute form of paralysis that's unique to lightning strikes—and thankfully temporary. Do your best to keep him or her reassured and warm until medical assistance arrives.

MISSING CLOTHES A strike can blow off your clothes. A blanket will help with warmth—and modesty.

040

STEP-BY-STEP
Install Lightning Rods

A lightning bolt is as dangerous to your home as it is deadly to your body. Luckily, a lightning rod can protect that home from strikes—and the electrical shortages and fires that come with them. So buy some lightning rod kits at a home-maintenance store and install them on your roof.

STEP ONE Measure your perimeter to figure out how many poles you need. For every 100 feet (30 m) of your home's perimeter, you'll need one rod.

STEP TWO Walk around your house, looking for good places to put grounding plates. (Every rod you install will require a grounding plate.) You'll want to put them at opposite corners of the house, if possible.

STEP THREE For each grounding plate, dig a hole 3 feet (1 m) deep and 1 foot (30 cm) larger in diameter than the plate. Make sure the holes are at least 2 feet (60 cm) away from the external wall.

STEP FOUR Climb up onto your roof and, above each grounding plate, place a lightning rod at the roof's edge. The rods should be 20 feet (6 m) away from each other and within 2 feet (60 cm) of the edge of the roof.

STEP FIVE Using a power drill, make holes in the exterior wall for the clamp that will hold the lightning rod to the roof.

STEP SIX Place the rod in the clamp and secure it to the exterior wall with screws.

STEP SEVEN Connect the conductor cable to the lightning rod, then run it down the exterior wall to the grounding plate below. Every 3 feet (1 m), use cable clamps to attach the cable to the wall.

STEP EIGHT Attach the conductor cable to the ground plate and secure it by tightening the screws on the support clamp. Finally, cover the plate with dirt.

Store firewood away from your home.

Avoid planting conifers.

Cover earth with mulch, gravel, or high-moisture plants.

Grow fire-resistant plants near your house.

Keep plants moist with drip irrigation.

Clear away low-hanging branches and deadwood near your home.

Install a spark arrester on your chimney.

Cover external vents with fine-mesh screens.

Protect Your Home from Wildfires

Firescaping is landscaping that's designed to keep your house from going up in smoke. Always a good investment, right?

PLANT WISELY Start by choosing the right kind of trees to plant. Conifers often contain flammable, sometimes explosive oils and resins. Trees that bear leaves are usually a safer bet. Protect your structures with fire-resistant, high-moisture vegetation like ice plant. Use a drip-irrigation system to water trees and shrubs year-round. Or use nonflammable ground cover such as mulch and gravel.

TRIM YOUR TREES Make sure to maintain the trees within 30 feet (9 m) of your home by trimming dead or low-hanging branches, which will be the first to light up. While you're keeping dry wood away from the house, make sure your woodpile is set back a good distance, too.

COVER UP Cover external vents with a fine-mesh screen to keep embers from blowing in. Consider installing chimney caps, which keep embers from a wildfire out—and those from your fireplace in.

042

Prevent a Forest Fire

Smokey the Bear doesn't like it when your campfire gets away from you—especially if it ends up torching the forest.

PICK A SPOT THAT HAS BURNED BEFORE The most safe place that you can build a fire is in an existing fire pit, since surrounding flammable materials have already burned.

START FROM SCRATCH If you have to build a fresh fire base, look for a site that's at least 15 feet (5 m) from bushes, dry grasses, and other flammable objects. Avoid overhead foliage, too. Clear a spot 10 feet (3 m) in diameter, removing twigs, leaves, and anything else that can burn. Dig a pit in the soil 1 foot (30 cm) deep. Circle the pit with rocks. When you're done with the fire, pour water on it or use dirt to smother the embers.

043 Survive a Wildfire

During a wildfire, the most dangerous places to be are uphill or downwind from the flames. Speaking of wind, if it's blowing toward the fire, run into the wind. But if it's behind the fire, you need to move away even faster—that fire will be coming on quick.

If told to evacuate, do so. But if you're trapped at home, stay inside where the structure will protect you. Move to a central room, away from the exterior walls of your house. Close the doors in order to cut down on air circulation, which can feed the flames.

If you're caught in the open, move to an area that has already burned over. Avoid canyons and other natural chimneys. Get into a river or lake, if possible. Look for breaks in the trees, which could mean breaks in the firestorm. If you're near a road, lie facedown along the road or in a ditch or depression on the uphill side. Cover up with anything that provides a shield against the heat.

044

Withstand a Firestorm

On October 25, 2003, Jacqueline Lloyd noticed a plume of smoke rising from a hill near her family's farm outside San Diego, California. Fires were not uncommon in the area, but usually firefighters' helicopters quickly arrived to quench them with water. After half an hour, Lloyd did not hear the reassuring sound of helicopters, so she called emergency services.

The dispatcher told her that the fire had been reported, so she shouldn't worry about it. But Jacqueline kept monitoring the emergency-band scanner she'd bought for just such an occasion. She and her husband also kept watch from the roof of the house. Several hours later, they saw that the fire was spreading in all four directions.

At that point they had to decide if they should trust that firefighters would extinguish the blaze before it reached them, or if they should pack up their 18-month-old child and various animals and flee to a relative's house. When a high-wind forecast was announced on the scanner, the Lloyds knew things would get worse. The Santa Ana winds were blowing the flames toward their home.

During the next hour, the Lloyds packed irreplaceable mementos like home movies and photo albums. They loaded everything in the car, along with their pets. But as they tried to load their horses into their trailers, the animals panicked. By

that stage, a wall of fire was roaring toward the barn, so the Lloyds turned the horses loose to follow their own instincts. Jacqueline Lloyd drove off with her daughter and pets, leaving her husband behind to run through the house one last time, using a video recorder to document their belongings for insurance purposes.

With her daughter tucked into the car seat beside her, she raced through winding roads rimmed with fire and choked with dense smoke. They arrived at the agreed-upon rendezvous point: her mother-in-law's home at the bottom of the canyon, where other family members had also evacuated.

The fire was fast approaching, but no one could see it clearly because of the canyon walls. Then her husband arrived with terrifying news: The fire had jumped the road just half a mile away. This finally convinced the family to leave the area entirely.

Despite the fact that they waited until the last moment to evacuate, Lloyd and her family all survived the fire. Their animals (including the horses left behind) made it through as well. Their mother-in-law's ranch house burned to the ground, and the Lloyds lost part of their home, their outbuildings, and their barn. They were lucky: 120 people were hurt, 14 residents and one firefighter were killed, and 2,000 homes were lost.

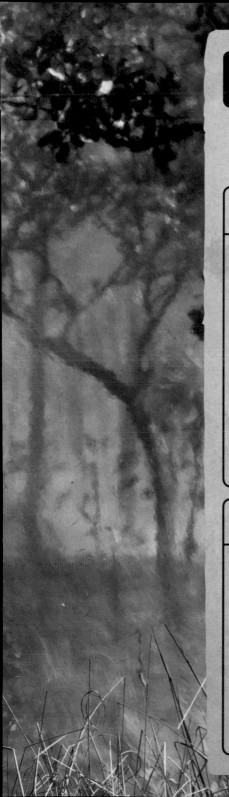

When Things Get Hot

A hunter who was lost in the California mountains built a signal fire, which spread until it destroyed thousands of homes and killed 15 people. The Lloyd family narrowly escaped.

 Jacqueline Lloyd spotted the fire while it was still small and called 911 to report it.

The Lloyds had purchased a fire scanner, and used it to monitor dispatches and keep up-to-date on the latest conditions.

They understood the weather conditions and the impact they were having on the fire.

Once the horses balked, the Lloyds released them rather than wasting time trying to coax them into their trailers.

Jacqueline and her husband set a rendezvous point in case they had to separate.

When the Lloyds and other family members arrived at the rendezvous point, they stayed together and monitored emergency reports.

When the fire jumped the road a half mile away, the Lloyds convinced everyone to evacuate.

 Although the Lloyds felt threatened, they only evacuated after an official order.

When they realized they had to leave, they spent time packing nonessential items.

Despite having been through a previous fire, the Lloyds did not have an evacuation plan.

Their desire to protect their horses put them in danger as they tried to evacuate the animals.

They nearly stayed too long in both locations, waiting until the fire was physically upon them before racing away.

The Lloyds spent a lot of time documenting possessions for insurance purposes rather than focusing on saving their own lives.

045 Survive a Volcanic Eruption

When the earth blows its top, the dangers include fiery lava bombs lobbed by the eruption, a tide of molten rock, and the toxic fumes of pyroclastic gas flows.

HIT THE ROAD, JACK The safest place to be is far away. Distance is the best protection against the fury and hellfire of a volcano, so be ready to evacuate when the warning is issued.

TAKE SHELTER If you can't put space between you and the eruption, find shelter and cross your fingers. A house can provide protection from ash and falling debris, but then again, it could catch on fire. So if you shelter inside, be ready to hustle out fast. Taking shelter inside a vehicle also might protect against some dangers. Since things that flow go downhill, wherever you hole up, make sure it's not in a low-lying area.

046 Cope with Ash

Volcanic ash isn't soft and fluffy—as if the mountain had been in a pillow fight. Nope, ash is composed of tiny jagged pieces of rock and glass. It's hard, abrasive, and corrosive. Because it destroys engines when it's sucked into the intake, volcanic ash halts air travel and hampers ground transportation for hundreds of miles around an eruption. But if you live close to an active volcano, your problems might be much more immediate than travel delays.

TAKE COVER During an ash fall, stay inside—especially if you have a respiratory ailment. Close doors, windows, vents, and chimney flues. Monitor radio and TV broadcasts about the situation.

WEAR LAYERS If you have to go outside, wear long sleeves and pants. Breathe through a dust mask, or hold a damp cloth over your nose and mouth. Use goggles or wear eyeglasses instead of contact lenses to avoid trapping dust and ash beneath them.

START SHOVELING Ash accumulations can pile deep on roofs, requiring shovel work to prevent them from collapsing. Make sure you clear rain gutters as well.

BE CAREFUL ON THE ROAD Prevent engine damage by avoiding driving. If you must, drive slowly and bear in mind that some roads may be impassable.

047 Assess a Lava Field

Even if you're pretty sure it has cooled and hardened, it's better to detour around a lava field—because if you're wrong, you're toast. Literally.

TREAD LIGHTLY If you must cross, try to ensure that the lava has totally hardened. You can't always tell from looking, because molten lava might be flowing below a thin crust that can fool you. As you move forward, probe the ground ahead of you with a stick.

DO A SNIFF TEST Pay attention to air quality. Sulfur dioxide gases indicate flowing lava beneath you. This gives you two reasons to get away: Not only is the ground unstable, but that gas is toxic as well.

HEED YOUR FEET If the soles of your boots start to melt, the flow is definitely too hot to walk on. And if the ground feels at all mushy, that means it's too unstable to cross.

048 Retrofit Your House

Live in an area with a lot of seismic activity? Then make sure your house is as close to earthquake-proof as possible by getting it retrofitted. While it's not a guarantee that the Big One won't do a lot of damage, retrofitting helps keep your home anchored to the concrete pad or foundation it's sitting on—even when the earth under it is moving. This task is best left to pros, because it's complex and requires expertise.

BOLT IT DOWN Sandwiched between your house and its concrete foundation is a layer of wood called a "mudsill." Most likely, your home is already bolted down through this mudsill into the foundation, but in retrofitting, these fasteners are checked and replaced if necessary. Then bolts are added to help keep your house locked down tight.

BRACE THE CRIPPLE WALLS Take a look at your home's foundation. Chances are, there's a short wall between the concrete and the floor. This support is called a "cripple wall," and it's usually the first thing to collapse in an earthquake, making your home shift dramatically or even fall. You (or your contractor) can reinforce cripple walls by adding plywood panels to both sides of the support.

USE BRACKETS These days, most homes have shear walls, composed of braced panels that resist lateral movement. These are great, but you or the pro you hire might want to reinforce them with angled hold-down brackets. These brackets are made to prevent shear walls from lifting up out of the foundation during a major seismic event.

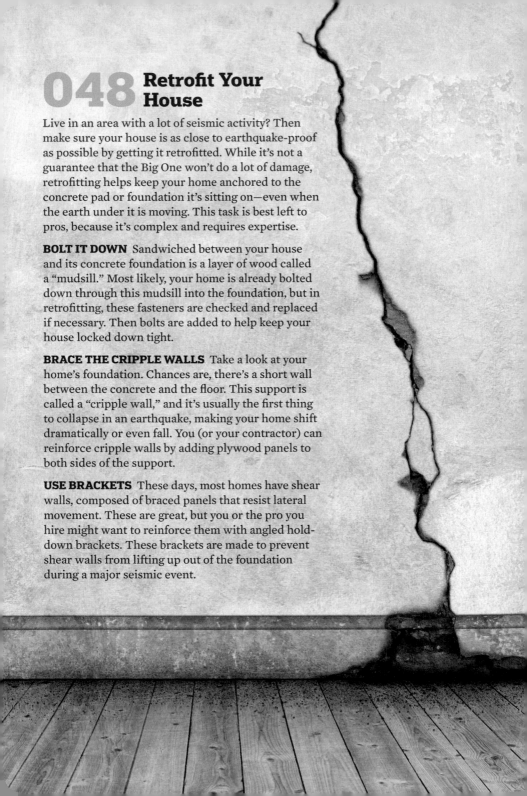

049

Keep Household Items Steady in a Quake

When there's a whole lot of shakin' going on, there could be a whole lot of falling. And smashing. And crashing. Here's how to keep your home and its contents from tumbling down around or on you in an earthquake. (All the items mentioned here are readily available in home-furnishing and hardware stores.)

BATTEN DOWN THE BIG STUFF Strap water heaters to the wall with perforated metal strips known as plumber's tape. Make sure that all piping is flexible rather than rigid, and insert a nonflammable spacer between the heater and the wall. For refrigerators and large appliances, use an L-bracket to bolt the top to the wall. To secure your fridge's bottom to the floor, use pronged Z-clips.

MAKE SURE FURNITURE IS FIXED IN PLACE Secure large objects such as cabinets, bookcases, and hutches to the wall using L-brackets or furniture-securing kits. Equip all cabinets with latches to keep their contents from spilling out.

STOP THE SHATTERING Apply clear polyester sheets to help keep windows and mirrors from breaking. You can pick some up at a home-supply store.

BEWARE OF WALL HANGINGS Place heavier ornamental items like mirrors or paintings only on walls well away from beds and seating areas. Don't count on a hook and nail to hold them in place—use wall anchors instead.

REARRANGE DISPLAYS Move heavy objects to lower shelves so they'll do less damage if they're shaken loose. Place objects with low centers of gravity, like fishbowls and vases, on nonstick mats to help keep them from shifting too.

SWEAT THE SMALL STUFF Apply earthquake putty to the bottom of small items so they won't move.

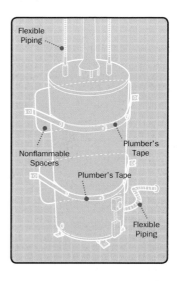

Flexible Piping

Nonflammable Spacers

Plumber's Tape

Plumber's Tape

Flexible Piping

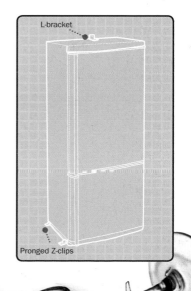

L-bracket

Pronged Z-clips

050

Know Earthquake Hot Spots

Of the 500,000 tremors that occur every year, we only feel about 100,000. Sometimes, though, one will cause extreme loss of life and structural damage. Luckily, we know where they are likely to strike:

PACIFIC RING OF FIRE More than 80 percent of the world's worst quakes occur on this fault system.

ALPIDE BELT This volatile area is the second most dangerous quake zone in the world.

CAYMAN TRENCH This system of fault lines exists between the North American and Caribbean plates.

ANYONE'S GUESS Some quakes can occur well within a plate's boundaries. These intraplate quakes often cause more damage, as buildings in those areas are not retrofitted.

Kuril-Kamchatka Trench (Russia)
9.0 quake in 1952

Chaman Fault (Afghanistan)
7.7 quake in 1935

⊛ ALPIDE BELT

Gujarat Fault (India)
7.7 quake in 2001

Sunda Megathrust Fault
(Sumatra)
9.1 quake in 2004

051 Understand Fault Activity

The plates making up our planet's topmost crust are in a constant game of push and shove. Often those plates get stuck together along fault lines, where they store up tension. Eventually, though, something has to give, and the pent-up energy radiates in seismic waves that we feel up above. That's how you get an earthquake.

An earthquake's magnitude is affected by many factors. In general, the longer the fault line, the larger the quake. Tremors that occur fewer than 43 miles (70 km) underground are deemed "shallow" quakes, and they're more likely to cause dramatic effects on land. Lastly, there are three main types of faults along which earthquakes occur . . . and some create worse quakes than others.

What determines an earthquake's intensity? That has much to do with the population density of an affected area, as well as the area's geology: Places with loose soil and rocks are more prone to sliding. Of course, the better a community prepares itself through retrofitting and smart construction, the better off it will be in the event of a quake.

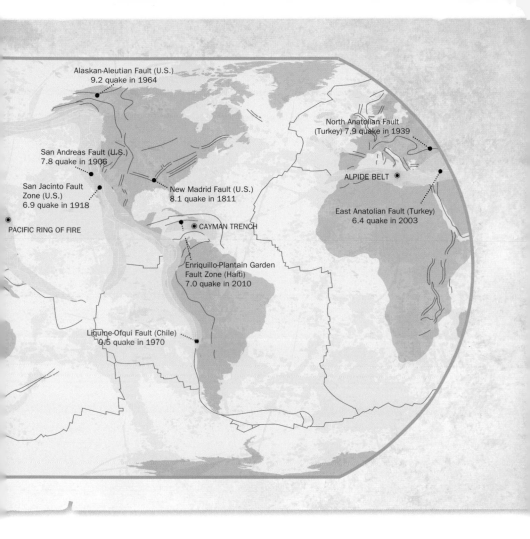

Alaskan-Aleutian Fault (U.S.)
9.2 quake in 1964

North Anatolian Fault
(Turkey) 7.9 quake in 1939

San Andreas Fault (U.S.)
7.8 quake in 1906

San Jacinto Fault
Zone (U.S.)
6.9 quake in 1918

New Madrid Fault (U.S.)
8.1 quake in 1811

ALPIDE BELT

East Anatolian Fault (Turkey)
6.4 quake in 2003

CAYMAN TRENCH

PACIFIC RING OF FIRE

Enriquillo-Plantain Garden
Fault Zone (Haiti)
7.0 quake in 2010

Liquine-Ofqui Fault (Chile)
9.5 quake in 1970

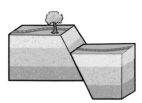

NORMAL FAULTS are also called divergent faults. When pieces of land on opposite sides of a fault pull away from each other, tremors of up to 7.0 magnitude result.

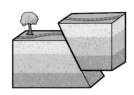

REVERSE FAULTS exist where opposite sides push against one another. Reverse faults are the most deadly, creating earthquakes that hit 8.0 on the Richter scale.

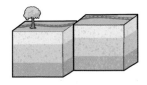

STRIKE-SLIP FAULTS occur where the sides move laterally against each other. Left-lateral faults displace land on the left, while right-lateral faults displace on the right.

052 Ride Out a Quake in a Car

You probably know the drill: If you're inside a building when an earthquake hits, stay there. If you're outside, get into a clearing. But what if you're driving?

STOP FOR THE SHAKING There are two hazards if an earthquake strikes when you're driving: other drivers and falling objects. Pull over in an area free of things that might fall on your car, such as telephone poles, street lights, and, yes, even overpasses. The more open the area, the safer it is.

DEAL WITH INFRASTRUCTURE If you're on a bridge, take the next exit off it. And if you're stuck under that overpass, get out of your car and lie flat beside it. Should the structure collapse, it will crush your car, but not to the ground—which will hopefully leave a safe zone immediately around your vehicle.

HEAD HOME There is always a chance of aftershocks, so don't hurry off. Listen to the radio for updates that may affect your route, and expect accidents and damage.

053 Survive Being Trapped Under Debris

See a clear path to safety? Then get yourself out. But when the walls come down, people inside usually can't save themselves. Let rescuers know where you are by tapping on a pipe or wall. Use a whistle if you have one. To avoid inhaling dust, cover your mouth and nose with a cloth, and use your voice only as a last resort. Don't light a match or lighter to see where you are, as there could be a gas leak.

054 Weather an Earthquake

A surprising number of people—including those in quake-prone regions, who should take a keen interest in the topic—don't know what to do when the shaking starts. But a little foresight could save your life.

TAKE COVER Assess every room you spend time in and pick the spot that's likely to be safest in a quake. For instance, if your office has a sturdy desk, you might want to follow the classic "duck, cover, and hold" advice by diving under the desk and holding on to its legs. Stay there until the shaking stops.

DO GEOMETRY Nothing sturdy enough to protect you from falling rubble (which could include fragments of the ceiling)? Use the "triangle of life" tactic and crouch beside a large, stable piece of furniture that could deflect debris.

Or cover your face and head, and stoop in an inside corner of the building that's away from possible falling objects.

GET CLEAR If you're outside when a quake hits, head to an open space that's away from structures, streetlights, and overhead wires. The area of highest risk is directly outside buildings.

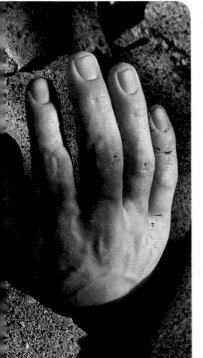

055 Take Action After an Earthquake

Surviving the shake doesn't mean you're out of the woods. What you choose to do immediately after an earthquake is just as important as what you're doing during the event.

PREVENT FIRE If the building you're in appears to be structurally sound, open doors and windows to ventilate gas fumes or dust. Avoid using any gas or electrical appliances, since the greatest danger after an earthquake is fire.

PROTECT YOURSELF Before you go running out into the street, put on boots or shoes with heavy soles, and find a pair of sturdy gloves to wear. Both can help you avoid sharp objects and potential electrical hazards.

MAKE AN ESCAPE If you're leaving a multistory building, be aware that stairwells may have shifted. Descend slowly so you can be sure of your footing. and don't run: It could disturb and weaken the stairs further.

THIS HAPPENED TO ME!
Tsunami Race

IT WAS OUR HONEYMOON, AND BRETT AND I WERE RELAXING ON A BEACH IN INDONESIA WHEN SUDDENLY THE WATER IN THE BAY RUSHED OUT. WE KNEW SOMETHING WAS WRONG.

I PULLED ON BRETT'S ARM, REALIZING THAT WHAT WENT OUT MUST SURELY BE COMING BACK.

IT WAS A TSUNAMI!

WE THOUGHT WE WERE SAFE WHEN WE MADE IT TO THE COURTYARD A COUPLE STORIES UP FROM THE BEACH.

BUT THEN WE SAW THE SECOND WAVE COMING UP OVER THE LEDGE!

WE INCHED OUR WAY ALONG THE WALL AS THE COURTYARD FILLED WITH WATER. OUR ONLY HOPE WAS TO MAKE IT TO THE BALCONY.

WHEN IT LOOKED LIKE ALL WOULD BE LOST, A STRANGER REACHED DOWN FROM THE BALCONY TO HELP PULL US UP TO SAFETY.

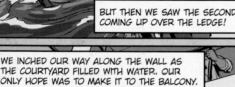
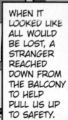

EVEN ON THE BALCONY, WE FELT LIKE WE WERE IN DANGER, SO WE MADE OUR WAY TO THE ROOF.

FROM THE TOP OF THE BUILDING, WE COULD SEE HOW WIDESPREAD THE DAMAGE WAS. OUR HONEYMOON HAD ALMOST TURNED INTO THE LAST TRIP OF OUR LIVES.

057

Brace for a Big Wave

It's not just earthquakes that cause tsunamis: Volcanic activity, landslides, or impact from space objects can all set one off. And since the biggest tsunamis are as tall as 100 feet (30 m), you'll want to get at least that high above sea level. Any time you're in a coastal area, think about where you would go in a big-wave emergency.

PLOT YOUR ESCAPE Do a little recon to identify escape routes to high ground. Plan on following designated tsunami evacuation routes (if they're established in your area) or simply heading inland and uphill as quickly as possible.

STAY TUNED Keep your ear tuned to the radio and TV for warnings. Evacuate immediately upon receiving notice of an impending tsunami.

GET THE HECK OUT Unless you have a death wish, don't go to the beach to watch the waves come ashore. Immediately meet up with your loved ones and head for high ground.

056 Know Tsunami Warning Signs

A tsunami can travel through deep water at more than 600 miles per hour (965 km/h), crossing an ocean in less than a day. And it won't calm down when it hits shore: Shallower water actually makes it taller. Here's how to tell if a big wave is headed your way.

A MAJOR SHAKE-UP An earthquake in a coastal region is an obvious warning sign. If you live near the earthquake, seek out high ground. Even if the earthquake is across the ocean, monitor broadcasts for warnings—tsunamis can travel long distances.

ANTSY ANIMALS Look out for changes in animal behavior. Scientists believe critters pick up on the earth's vibrations before we do, so if they're nervous, it may be for good reason.

RECEDING WATER The first part of a tsunami to reach land is the drawback trough, which causes coastal waters to recede, exposing those normally submerged areas. If you're seeing a drawback, you've got about five minutes before the big wave hits.

058 Deal with a Tsunami at Sea

Strange but true: One of the safest places to be during an earthquake-triggered tsunami is on a boat in deep water. A quake beneath the ocean floor produces a powerful energy impulse that races horizontally through the water, but in the deep ocean that energy flows through without disturbing the surface. It's when that energy meets the shallows that the water rises up into a wave.

If you're on a boat in a harbor and you learn that a tsunami is coming, either immediately head for deeper water or abandon the boat and get to high ground. If you're on your way to deep water and the first wave catches you, steer the boat up the wave and apply maximum throttle to climb the swell. Keep heading for deeper water until the entire event has passed.

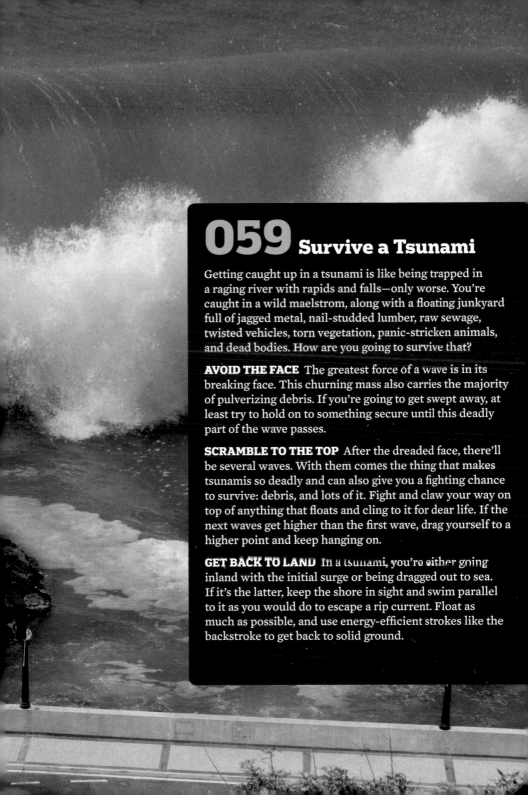

059 Survive a Tsunami

Getting caught up in a tsunami is like being trapped in a raging river with rapids and falls—only worse. You're caught in a wild maelstrom, along with a floating junkyard full of jagged metal, nail-studded lumber, raw sewage, twisted vehicles, torn vegetation, panic-stricken animals, and dead bodies. How are you going to survive that?

AVOID THE FACE The greatest force of a wave is in its breaking face. This churning mass also carries the majority of pulverizing debris. If you're going to get swept away, at least try to hold on to something secure until this deadly part of the wave passes.

SCRAMBLE TO THE TOP After the dreaded face, there'll be several waves. With them comes the thing that makes tsunamis so deadly and can also give you a fighting chance to survive: debris, and lots of it. Fight and claw your way on top of anything that floats and cling to it for dear life. If the next waves get higher than the first wave, drag yourself to a higher point and keep hanging on.

GET BACK TO LAND In a tsunami, you're either going inland with the initial surge or being dragged out to sea. If it's the latter, keep the shore in sight and swim parallel to it as you would do to escape a rip current. Float as much as possible, and use energy-efficient strokes like the backstroke to get back to solid ground.

060 Know When Mud Might Flow

Mudslides occur when sloping ground becomes so saturated with water that the soil loses its grip and gravity takes over. Then you get to deal with a filthy deluge that can destroy your property and put your life at risk. Be smart and heed these warning signs:

KNOW THE STORY Contact local authorities for the geographical history of your area, including any fires that destroyed vegetation (leading to soil erosion) or construction that altered water flow.

AVOID EXTREME INCLINES Steep slopes that are close to the edge of a mountain range or valleys are bad news. If you can, simply live somewhere else that's less vulnerable.

WATCH THE WATER Take note of the patterns of storm-water drainage on slopes. Sudden changes in nearby streams can also indicate an impending slide.

MIND THE GAPS Cracks in pavement and walls pulling away from buildings mean that the land is moving, and may be vulnerable to mudslides. Beware cracks in your home's foundation, or if doors or windows start to stick in their frames.

LOOK FOR CROOKED STUFF Leaning trees or utility poles aren't charming quirks. The soil is eroding, and you should watch out.

061 Make It Through a Mudslide

Earthquakes, volcanic eruptions, heavy rainstorms, or just plain old erosion all can start a mudslide. However they start, they're always a dirty bad time.

STAY AWAKE Most mudslide-related deaths occur at night, when people are asleep. If the rain is coming down hard and flooding and slides are predicted, put on a pot of coffee and continue to monitor weather and evacuation reports.

LISTEN FOR THE RUMBLE Mudslides don't just come crashing down silently. If you hear a rumbling sound coming from up the hill, evacuate immediately.

GET OUT OF THE SLIDE'S PATH Sometimes there's no time to evacuate. If you're caught in a mudslide, the best you can do is try to move out of its way. If it's too late, curl into a tight ball and fold your arms over your head for protection.

062

STEP-BY-STEP
Save Your Home from Mudslides

To prevent your dream home from turning into a muddy nightmare, take these steps.

STEP ONE If you suspect your house may be in a slide zone, have a geological assessment done. Better yet, do that before you buy the home.

STEP TWO Consider the drainage on your property. If your home or yard often floods, use gravity to direct water away from your foundation. Dig a trench 1 to 2 feet (30–60 cm) deep and equally wide, and line it with compacted limestone.

STEP THREE A vertical retaining wall acts as a buffer and prevents land from sliding down a hill—taking your home with it. A good rule of thumb is to build a system of walls no more than 2 feet (60 cm) high, staggered down the hillside. Provide drainage behind the walls, or the soil will erode and destabilize them.

STEP FOUR Topsoil needs strongly rooted vegetation to keep it in place. Begin with a solid carpeting of sod, followed by trees and faster-growing shrubs such as privets or decorative perennials like roses.

KNOW THE NUMBERS
Mudslides

130 square miles (300 sq km) Largest area covered by a mudslide.

738 billion gallons (2.792 trillion l) Largest volume of mud from a single slide in modern times.

23,000 Largest confirmed mudslide death toll, caused by a 1985 slide in Colombia.

30,000 Largest estimated death toll for a single mudslide, which happened in Venezuela in 1999.

$1.79 billion to $3.5 billion Estimated damage costs from the 1999 mudslide in Vargas, Venezuela.

More than 90 Percentage of mudslides triggered by heavy rainfall.

35 Percentage of mudslides influenced by human activities such as scrub clearing and building construction.

210 Average number of yearly landslide events that impact human beings.

30 to 50 miles per hour (48–80 km/h) Average spoeed of a mudslide.

200 miles per hour (320 km/h) Fastest recorded speed of a mudslide.

063 Know You're in Avalanche Country

When a layer of snow breaks loose upslope and roars down the mountain at 200 miles per hour (321 km/h), it buries everything in its path. To avoid becoming a human Popsicle, learn to recognize the danger signs.

WATCH THE WEATHER Avalanche risks increase after a heavy snowfall. The most precarious time of all is when snowy weather is followed by warm weather or rain—and then cold, snowy conditions return.

MEASURE THE SLOPE Avalanches mostly occur when the slope is 30 to 45 degrees, but even slopes of 25 to 60 degrees can slide if conditions are right (or, from your perspective, very wrong).

SEEK THE SUN Snow is most volatile on slopes that face away from the sun during winter, so try to plan a route that keeps you off them.

STEP AROUND MOUNDS Watch out for areas where the wind has piled snow high (especially at the tops of mountains, gullies, and canyons).

RECOGNIZE BAD SNOW Don't tread on snow that makes a hollow sound when you step on it or on snow that looks like large, sparkly crystals instead of powder—this is deadly stuff called "depth hoar."

LOOK FOR WRECKAGE Snow debris and broken trees are signs of previous avalanches, so be especially wary of these trouble spots.

BEWARE OF CHUTES Vegetation and boulders act as anchors for snowpack. If there are no trees or rocks on a slope, then it's a big amusement-park ride for snow—and you don't want to be on it.

WATCH FOR TRIGGERS A loud noise or tumbles taken by skiers or snowboarders can activate avalanches. Be wary if you see any of these catalysts.

STAY SAFE Some avalanches strike with no warning, so err on the safe side. If you're hiking, stick to ridgelines, windward hillsides, dense forests, or low-angle slopes. If you're skiing, stay on groomed trails.

064 Assess Incline

We all know that most avalanches start on slopes with an angle of 30 to 45 degrees, so these are the ones to avoid at all costs. But how do you figure out the angle?

If you're an avid mountaineer, you might want to invest in an inclinometer—a reasonably priced tool that measures the slope exactly. If you're not a backcountry hiker, skier, or hunter, that's probably overkill. Instead, tie a small weight to a string (one of the cords on your parka will do), dangle it to touch the snow's surface, and eyeball the slope's angle: A right angle is 90 degrees, so half of that is a dangerous 45-degree angle, and if you see that, you'd better move it. High-school geometry does come in handy after all.

065 Recognize Avalanche Types

Understanding the conditions that cause avalanches will help you avoid them—and trust me, you definitely want to avoid them.

SLAB AVALANCHES These bad boys account for more than 90 percent of avalanche fatalities. Slab avalanches don't generate from a single point, which might allow a skier or hiker to move laterally out of the way. Instead, an entire sheet of snow—sometimes a massively wide one—gives way at once. Slab avalanches happen when a thick layer of dense snow settles on top of looser snow.

LOOSE-SNOW SLIDES Also called "sluffs", these are the least dangerous avalanche types, but they often injure skiers and snowboarders by causing them to change course and head into dangerous terrain. Sluffs occur in cold, dry conditions, when the snow is powdery and lacks cohesion.

WET AVALANCHES These avalanches tend to move more slowly than dry avalanches, but they present just as much danger. When temperatures are at or above freezing for a period of days, the surface snow melts and saturates the layers beneath it, making it prone to sliding. To check for wet-avalanche conditions, pick up a handful of snow and squeeze. If your glove gets very wet, it's best to take a different route.

066 Ride Out an Avalanche

Caught in an avalanche? Well, that's plain bad luck. Use skiing (or even surfing) moves to try to ride on top of the snow, and attempt to maneuver toward the edge of the slide. If the snow is moving slowly, try to catch hold of a tree without getting creamed by it. In a fast-moving slide that knocks you off your feet, swim in the snow and try to avoid hitting stationary obstacles.

067

Know Which Way Is Up

You might be able to dig out after an avalanche has tumbled and rolled you—but only if you know which direction is up. If the snow layer above you is relatively thin, light might shine through, so go toward that. If you're too deep for light to be your guide, clear a space near your mouth and spit. Watch the direction in which gravity pulls the spit, and head the other way.

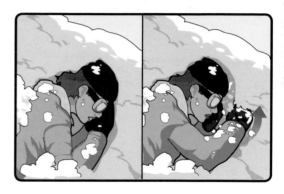

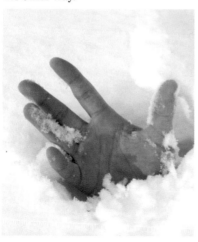

068

Get Rescued from an Avalanche

Being buried under the snow is not an enviable position. But it doesn't have to be a fatal one.

REACT QUICKLY Once the snow stops moving, it turns from a fluid medium to a cement-like consistency. So try to work your way to the surface as the slide slows.

SEEK THE SURFACE If possible, shove one arm toward the surface and move it around to create an air shaft. Use your hands to carve out a breathing space. Work methodically to avoid becoming exhausted.

DON'T SHOUT RANDOMLY Conserve your breath until you hear rescuers above you.

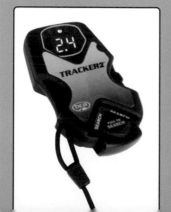

069 Strap On a Safety Beacon

If you're crazy enough to spend time in unstable snowscapes, you might want to invest in an avalanche beacon. Turn the unit on, set it to transmit, and strap it around your waist and over a shoulder under your outer layer of clothing. Let others know your plans prior to heading out. If you end up buried in a snowslide, rescuers will pick up your signal and know where to start digging.

070

Walk in a Whiteout

I have a friend who got lost between his house and barn because the snow was falling so fast that he couldn't see the ground—or the 100 feet (30 m) between the two structures. He survived getting lost in a whiteout. I hope you're as lucky.

RESPECT THE STORM Forget winter wonderland: A whiteout is a horror show. You can't imagine how disorienting it is until you're in one. So only venture out as a last resort—say, if you have to get to emergency gear, clear the hood of your car to keep it visible to rescuers, or help someone who is stranded a short distance away.

TIE YOURSELF TO HOME BASE One way to keep from getting totally lost in a whiteout is to tie one end of a long rope to your starting point and the other end around your waist. The rope doesn't help you reach your destination, but it will help you get back. (If you know a blizzard is coming, and you anticipate needing to travel back and forth between buildings, tie a rope between them before the snow starts.)

PROTECT YOUR FACE Cover your mouth and nose to shield them from the wind and snow. Heck, go ahead and cover your eyes, too, since you're definitely not using them to see.

071

Drive in a Blizzard

Driving in a snowstorm is like trying to steer with a pillowcase over your head. It's bad enough during daylight, but it gets really hairy at night when you turn on your headlights, since every snowflake reflects the light back into your eyes. And it's not only you: Everybody else out there is just as blind, too.

If a snowstorm escalates, pull to the side of the road. Reduce your beams to parking lights to aid your own vision, and use emergency flashers to help others see you. Above all, stay inside the vehicle so that you don't get hit by another car. When the weather does clear up and you think it's safe to drive away, clear snow out of your brake lights (so other drivers can see you) and off the top of the car (so the snow doesn't tumble down and impede visibility).

Chances are you'll also need to dig out your wheels to gain traction and get moving. Experienced winter drivers carry a shovel, as well as kitty litter or long pieces of wood. Lay these items down on the snow or ice in front of your wheels to help increase your vehicle's traction.

072 Survive in a Snowbound Car

If you're stuck in a blizzard, a vehicle can protect you from wind and snow, and its visibility ups the odds that a search crew will find you. But in bitter cold, your car can feel like a freezer, because metal and glass offer no insulation. The solution is the same as the problem: snow.

PILE IT ON If you are driving in snowy conditions, keep a shovel in the trunk. A foot of snow piled on the car's roof and trunk will turn it into a cozy-ish metal-lined snow cave.

HEAT THINGS UP Wear all the clothing you have in the car and run the heater in short bursts. Just don't use it constantly (you'll run out of gas), and clear snow from the exhaust pipe periodically to prevent carbon monoxide poisoning. If you happen to have a candle, light it up—it'll deliver an amazing amount of warmth.

STAY VISIBLE Keep snow off the car's hood so searchers can spot the color contrast from the air. Tying a colored strip of cloth to your vehicle's antenna can also get you noticed, and thus rescued, more quickly.

KEEP MOVING Exercise every so often inside the car to keep your circulation going. This will also keep you from falling asleep—which can be deadly if it's cold enough.

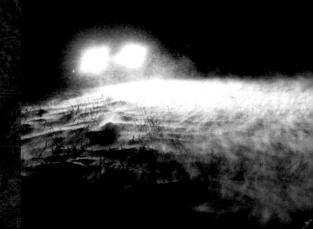

073

Ride Out a Blizzard at Home

Once a blizzard hits, all you can do is sit tight; there's no skipping out to the grocery for supplies when visibility is zero. Get your act together while the clouds are still gathering.

STOCK UP Make sure your at-home survival kit is well loaded with the usual essentials, plus extra blankets, sleeping bags, heavy coats, and warm clothing.

WATCH YOUR WATER Severe cold can freeze pipes, leaving you without water to drink or the ability to flush a toilet more than one last time. Store water in containers where it won't freeze.

REDECORATE STRATEGICALLY Hang quilts over windows for extra insulation. In the daytime, keep your curtains and blinds open to let sunlight warm up your home; shut them at night to keep heat in.

STAY WARM A storm might tear down power lines, and without electricity you can't operate a furnace. So get a generator or stock up on fuel for a wood-burning stove or fireplace. And if you're not on your own, huddle with others in a small room to combine and maximize your body heat.

074

STEP-BY-STEP
Store Food During a Blizzard

There's one upside to losing power in the winter: the ease with which you can store perishable food items. Essentially, the world is your freezer.

STEP ONE If there's a decent amount of snow covering the ground, dig yourself a cubby.

STEP TWO Direct contact with snow can damage meats and vegetables, and unpackaged food is also susceptible to hungry scavengers looking for an easy meal. It's best to put all perishable items into individual plastic bags to reduce odors that might otherwise attract hungry animals.

STEP THREE Store the packaged items in a wooden box or trunk (even a small side table with a latching door will work) and bury this item in the snow. You may end up losing a piece of furniture, but you'll prolong your food stores—and that trade-off is well worth the sacrifice.

075 Prevent Carbon Monoxide Poisoning

If you're snowed in without power, you'll have to improvise ways to cook and stay warm. Be careful, though, or you'll face a whole new problem: poisoning from carbon monoxide (CO).

CHECK THE METER Install a carbon monoxide detector in your home. It will alert you if levels of this odorless gas ever get dangerously high.

PREVENT THE PROBLEM Never bring a charcoal grill indoors for any reason. Even operating a propane lantern or stove indoors can raise the CO concentration to a dangerous level. Space heaters are notorious killers, especially when they're left running after everyone goes to bed.

KNOW THE SYMPTOMS Watch for common signs such as vertigo, fatigue, and headaches, as well as odd behavior. If more than one person in the house has these symptoms, you've got a problem.

BREATHE BETTER If you suspect that someone has been poisoned by CO, get everyone outdoors immediately and open the windows and doors to allow ventilation. For mild cases, fresh air is sufficient treatment. For serious cases, hyperbaric treatment at a medical facility may be needed.

FIX THE PROBLEM Discover the cause of the high concentration of CO and have the situation remedied. Call the fire department to test for safety.

076 STEP-BY-STEP Clear Heavy Snow

Folks who live in snow country know the value of a strong roof. A 1-inch (2.5-cm) layer of snow weighs approximately 5 pounds (2.25 kg) per square foot (.09 sq m)—and that can really add up. Sure, a little bit of snow can help insulate your home, but too much poses a hazard and should be removed.

STEP ONE Use an appropriate shovel with a longer handle for hard-to-reach areas. Start by clearing the apex of the roof, which will help you maintain a secure footing, and then work toward the edges.

STEP TWO Keep your gutters clear to avoid standing water—it will freeze in the cold, potentially causing structural damage to your home.

STEP THREE Don't forget tree branches, which heavy snow and ice can bring down; they may land on your home, a vehicle, a loved one, or a stranger passing by who happens to know a lawyer. Clear snow and ice by brushing it off the ends of limbs with a shovel, then work your way back to the trunk.

077

STEP-BY-STEP
Cover Your Face in a Sandstorm

When the wind whips up in the desert, you're likely to end up with a lot of sand in places you really don't want it to be. This simple mask will at least keep you from sucking in all the bad stuff.

STEP ONE Cut a strip of cloth (or a scarf, if you have one) 30 inches (76 cm) long. Fold it in half lengthwise.

STEP TWO Following the folded crease, cut a slit from both ends, each extending about a third of the way toward the center of the cloth.

STEP THREE Soak the cloth in water, then wring out the excess, but leave a little moisture.

STEP FOUR Place the center portion of the fabric over your chin, nose, and mouth.

STEP FIVE Tie the tails behind your head to secure the mask to your face.

078

Drive in a Sandstorm

Sand may not seem especially scary, but when the wind lifts it 50 feet (15 m) into the air and propels it at 75 miles per hour (120 km/h), it suddenly seems a lot fiercer than it does when you're at the beach. If you're on the road when a sandstorm hits, here are your options:

STOP If you observe dense sand blowing across the highway ahead, stop and wait for it to pass. But don't just halt on the pavement. Pull off the road as far as possible, turn off your lights, set the emergency brake, and take your foot off the brake pedal. This way, other drivers won't follow your lights and crash into you.

KEEP GOING If leaving the pavement is dangerous because of a drop-off or other obstacle, turn on your headlights, sound the horn periodically, and drive at a slow speed. Stay alert for other drivers doing the same. Don't turn off the road you're on, as it's easy to become disoriented in such low visibility.

079 Pick a Safe Seat on a Train

If a train slides off the rails or collides with something stubborn, things are likely to go seriously wrong. There won't be a great deal that you can do at the instant of impact, but you can take a few basic preemptive measures in order to reduce the risk of injury.

GO FOR THE MIDDLE The cars in the front and rear are the most likely to be involved in accidents. If you have a choice, stay off them.

SIT BACKWARD It might make you queasy, but try taking a seat that's facing away from the direction of travel. If the train crashes, you'll be pushed back into the seat—not thrown across the car.

AVOID OVERLOADING Find a seat that doesn't have much luggage in the overhead area, and store larger items in racks at the front of the car. In the event of an accident, at least those heavy items won't come tumbling down on you.

080 STEP-BY-STEP Stop a Train

Your train blows through your stop at lightning speed, and you realize you're not on the express—you're on a runaway train! (How do you keep getting yourself in these situations?) If it's up to you to stop the locomotive, try this:

STEP ONE Locate the emergency brake in your car and pull the cord.

STEP TWO If the train doesn't stop, head toward the engine up front. As you go from car to car, activate the individual friction brakes in each car, controlled by a wheel or lever, to help slow the train.

STEP THREE Once in the engine car, push the button labeled "E-brake" or "emergency brake." Lower the throttle handle to decrease speed, then find the dynamic brake handle and move it to "setup"—this will kill the throttle. Wait 5 seconds and move the brake handle to the highest position. Finally, locate the air-brake handle and move it to 100 percent.

STEP FOUR After you've applied the cockpit's various brakes, use the radio to call for help.

081 Get Your Car Off the Tracks

Car versus train never works out well—especially for the car. So never stop a vehicle on railroad tracks, and never race a train to the crossing. Play the lotto instead: You have a better chance of winning.

If, for some reason, your vehicle gets stuck on the tracks when no train is coming, go ahead and try to push or tow it off. Enlist help for this.

If you get any hint that even a distant train is on the way, is there anything to gain by staying? Let me answer that one for you: Nope! Run like crazy and get at least 200 feet (60 m) away, because parts of your beloved Camaro are about to become flying shrapnel.

082 Jump from a Moving Train

Unless you're riding an out-of-control train carrying explosives or hazardous materials, you're probably safer riding out a train wreck than attempting to jump while the train is moving. In a worst-case scenario, however, you've gotta do what you've gotta do, so at least prepare yourself for a rough landing.

LOOK BEFORE YOU LEAP Try to miss obvious obstacles, such as platforms, bridge infrastructure, posts, and trees. Aim to hit the ground on a soft, open spot.

ASSUME THE POSITION When you jump, hold your body in a slight crouch, bent at your knees and waist so you can absorb the blow. Keep your feet and knees together and your arms wrapped tightly across your chest, with your chin tucked. Try to hit the ground feet-first, then roll with the momentum.

1 Number of passengers killed in the first fatal aviation accident. It was in 1908, and Orville Wright was the pilot of the aircraft.

22 Percentage of aircraft fatalities caused by mechanical malfunction.

12 Percentage of fatalities that are entirely weather related.

1972 Year with the most airplane-accident deaths.

3,214 Number of air-travel-related fatalities in 1972.

083

Use Your Cell for an Airborne SOS

You aren't supposed to make calls on a cell phone during a commercial flight, because electromagnetic interference from the phone might adversely affect aircraft controls. However, if you can't reach the cockpit to use the radio—or if the radio's down—all bets are off. (That was certainly the case on September 11, 2001, when passengers on United Airlines Flight 93 placed emergency calls after terrorists took control of the plane.) As long as there's a cell tower in range, a mobile phone will work on a plane. The lower the plane's altitude, the greater the chances for a successful connection—and for getting assistance.

084 Contact Air Traffic Control

A quick hop on a small plane seems like a good idea—until the pilot starts clawing at his chest and turning blue.

CALL FOR HELP Make sure the radio is on and place your Mayday call on the frequency that's already set, since that's likely to be the one the local tower uses. If you need to select a frequency, try 121.5 MHz or 243.0 MHz, which air traffic control usually monitors.

LISTEN CAREFULLY The vast majority of successful landings by nonpilots are assisted by air traffic controllers. Many are pilots themselves, so they're likely to know how to get you down safely.

085 STEP-BY-STEP
Jump Out of an Airplane

Gravity is a drag, especially when you're falling out of an airplane without a parachute. If you're going to jump, you should use a chute.

STEP ONE Step into the harness so the leg-hole straps encircle your thighs, then bring the top straps over your shoulders and tighten the harness across your chest. Don't touch the rip cord before exiting the plane.

STEP TWO Jump from the airplane any way you can—except in front of an engine. If you think falling from a plane is bad, you should see what passing through a propeller or a turbine will do to ruin your day.

STEP THREE Count to three, then pull the rip cord.

STEP FOUR Plan your landing. Steer the parachute by pulling the handles, using the ones on your right to go right and those on your left to head left. Before landing, bend your knees, tuck in your elbows, and lower your chin to your chest. Roll with the landing.

THIS HAPPENED TO ME!
Panic in the Air

MY DAD HAD PROMISED AN AERIAL SIGHTSEEING TRIP, AND WE WERE FINALLY ON OUR WAY.

WE WERE BOTH EXCITED TO BE IN THE AIR. WE'D BEEN UP FOR A LITTLE MORE THAN AN HOUR WHEN OUR PILOT STARTED GASPING.

OH NO! HE'S HAVING A HEART ATTACK!

I WAS SCARED, BUT MY DAD TOOK CONTROL. WE MOVED THE PILOT TO THE FLOOR. I GAVE HIM ASPIRIN FROM MY PACK. DAD, MEANWHILE, HAD GOTTEN ON THE RADIO, CALLING THE AIRPORT WHERE WE'D TAKEN OFF.

WE WERE LUCKY THAT THE CONTROLLER WAS ALSO A PILOT. HE TALKED US THROUGH THE FIRST SCARY MOMENTS, WITH THE PILOT HELPING WHEN HE COULD. I COULDN'T BELIEVE DAD WAS FLYING US HOME!

BY THE TIME WE WERE READY TO LAND, OUR PILOT WAS ABLE TO GET BACK INTO THE CHAIR.

HE STILL NEEDED SOME HELP, THOUGH.

WHILE HE WORKED THE WHEEL, DAD HANDLED THE OTHER CONTROLS AS THE PILOT INSTRUCTED.

WHEN WE LANDED, WE WERE MET BY A FIRE TRUCK AND AN AMBULANCE, WHICH RUSHED OUR PILOT TO THE HOSPITAL. SURE, WE DIDN'T SEE MUCH FROM THE AIR, BUT WE ALL AGREED: WE'D HAD ENOUGH ADVENTURE FOR ONE DAY.

086
CHECKLIST
Salvage a Crash Site

After a plane crash, survivors face the challenge of staying alive until rescuers arrive. Depending on where the plane goes down, salvation might be only minutes away . . . or it could take days or even weeks for rescuers to find you. It's time to get creative.

☐ Check the cockpit for the plane's radio. If it works, send out a distress call.

☐ Use the fuselage as a shelter—that is, unless fuel has spilled, in which case there's a chance of fire, and you should move at least 100 feet (30 m) away.

☐ If the plane has broken up, put the cabin debris to good use: The carpeting, upholstery, seat cushions, bulkheads, overhead-bin doors, plastic windows, and aluminum can all become useful components of a temporary shelter.

☐ Dig through cargo compartments and luggage bins to find clothing, blankets, pillows, food, and water.

☐ Look for electrical wires, which you can use to lash together elements of your shelter.

☐ Punch a hole in the fuel tank (usually located in the wings of larger aircraft), drain the fuel into a container, and use it to start a fire.

☐ Use reflective materials for signal mirrors.

☐ Nearly all planes carry advanced medical supplies, including automatic defibrillators. Don't leave those critical items behind.

087 Make It to the Lifeboat

So you've boarded a fancy (or not so fancy) big boat and someone else is driving it. Great, but don't relax just yet. First note where the lifeboats and life jackets are stowed, and read the emergency card on the back of your stateroom door to learn the location of the lifeboat-muster area for your cabin. Then go find it.

If there's an evacuation drill, attend and pay attention. In an emergency, the captain will sound an alarm, consisting of seven short blasts followed by one long one. If your all-you-can-eat buffet is ever interrupted by this alarm (the horror!), make a beeline for the designated lifeboat-muster area and board the boat as instructed by ship personnel.

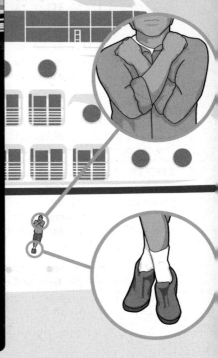

088 STEP-BY-STEP
Abandon Ship Safely

Unless you're the captain, you don't want to go down with the ship. Jumping off is no picnic, either, but if you must abandon ship, exit safely and quickly.

STEP ONE Avoid the crowd to keep from jostling for position, and move to the railing. If the ship is rolling, move to the high side so you aren't crushed by the boat if it capsizes. If you're 15 feet (5 m) above the water, it's too dangerous. Find a lower point or wait for the ship to sink further.

STEP TWO Look for a spot in the water that's free of debris and aim for it. It will take some courage, but when you've picked your spot, don't wait.

STEP THREE As you jump, cross your arms and grab your lapels, and cross your feet at the ankles—this will help prevent injuries from the impact. Take a big breath just before the splash.

STEP FOUR If you're close to a sinking ship, you risk being hurt by debris falling from the deck, so get well out of the way. Swim at least 100 feet (30 m) from the ship. Use either a sidestroke or backstroke to conserve energy, and be aware of obstacles or hazards.

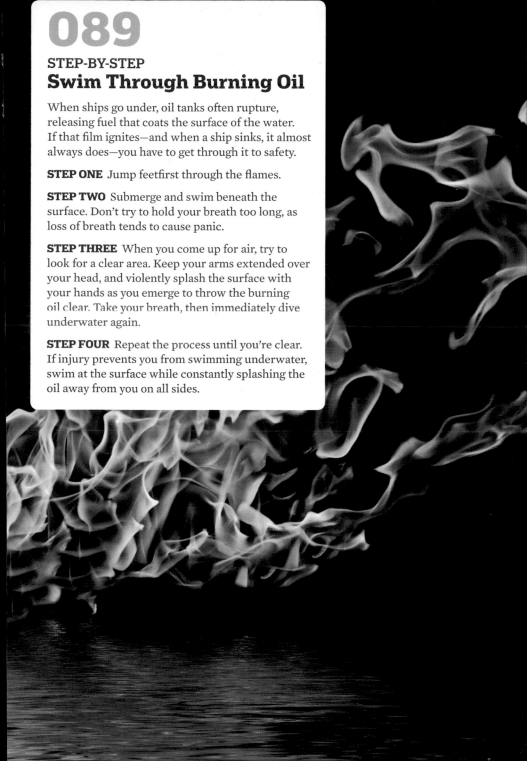

089

STEP-BY-STEP
Swim Through Burning Oil

When ships go under, oil tanks often rupture, releasing fuel that coats the surface of the water. If that film ignites—and when a ship sinks, it almost always does—you have to get through it to safety.

STEP ONE Jump feetfirst through the flames.

STEP TWO Submerge and swim beneath the surface. Don't try to hold your breath too long, as loss of breath tends to cause panic.

STEP THREE When you come up for air, try to look for a clear area. Keep your arms extended over your head, and violently splash the surface with your hands as you emerge to throw the burning oil clear. Take your breath, then immediately dive underwater again.

STEP FOUR Repeat the process until you're clear. If injury prevents you from swimming underwater, swim at the surface while constantly splashing the oil away from you on all sides.

090

Handle a Hazmat Situation

Hazmat situations usually involve noxious gases or explosive materials—hence the word "hazmat," which is short for "hazardous materials." These events are the real deal, so don't mess around.

STAY INFORMED Tune in to radio or TV broadcasts to stay up-to-date on the situation. If you're told to evacuate, do it as quickly as possible. Keep car windows shut as you flee the scene, and set your air conditioner to recirculate only.

AVOID THE DANGER ZONE If you're outdoors when the warning is issued, cover your face as much as possible and try stay upwind, uphill, and upstream of the hazmat location, preferably at least 1 mile (1.6 km) away. The source will most likely be an industrial facility, railway, or major highway.

091 Decontaminate Yourself

If you've been unlucky enough to get hazardous materials on yourself, you'd better act fast.

STEP ONE Immediately strip off your clothes and don't put them back on until they've been thoroughly laundered. This is no time for modesty—even a few seconds can make a big difference. While you're undressing, avoid touching your eyes, mouth, or nose, because you could be introducing dangerous chemicals into your system.

STEP TWO Rinse every affected area for at least fifteen minutes. If the material is flammable, brush it off before stepping under the showerhead.

STEP THREE If your luck is even worse and you do end up getting the bad stuff in your eyes, rinse them out as well, rolling your eyes back and forth under the stream to cleanse as much surface area as possible.

092
STEP-BY-STEP
Seal Your Home from a Toxic Spill

The instant you learn of a hazmat problem nearby, get indoors to limit exposure (unless you're told to evacuate). In especially bad cases, authorities may advise sealing your home. Here's how:

STEP ONE Shut any vents leading to the outside, including the fireplace damper. Turn off all air conditioners, fans, and ventilation systems.

STEP TWO Use plastic sheeting and duct tape to seal windows and doors. You can use aluminum foil or even wax paper to seal around air conditioner vents, kitchen and bathroom exhaust fans, and clothes dryer-vents.

STEP THREE Even outlets and light switches let in fumes. Tape them up, too.

STEP FOUR Close and lock exterior doors and windows so that no one can enter or leave after you seal the house.

STEP FIVE Move to an interior room. Once you're inside with all needed supplies, seal off conduits into the room with duct tape, close all interior doors, and place towels at the bottom of doors to limit the air circulation in the house.

093
Get Clear of a Hazard

Suddenly, a chemical facility in your area starts spewing smoke. Yikes. It's always a good idea to run, but it's also important to know when you're far enough away from the event to be safe. One nifty trick is literally a rule of thumb.

Spot the incident site and extend your arm toward it. Line up your thumb with the site; if you can obscure the entire area with your thumb, then you're at a safe distance for the moment. If your thumb doesn't cover it and the wind is blowing in your direction, then start sprinting: You need more distance between yourself and that toxic inferno, stat.

094 STEP-BY-STEP
Don a Gas Mask

Few things are more terrifying than a chemical or biological attack. Learning how to quickly don a gas mask and ensure a proper seal could be the difference between life and death. In an attack, you'll likely only have seconds to reach your mask and put it on, so practice until it's second nature.

STEP ONE With your thumbs on the inside of the mask, hold it by the sides. Insert your chin first, then pull the mask over your face and remove your thumbs.

STEP TWO Holding the mask in place with one hand, pull the straps over your head as far as possible, then tighten them from the top down. The mask should fit snugly and not move when you shake your head.

STEP THREE Place the palm of your hand over the filter or air intake, and breathe deeply until the mask seals tightly to your face.

STEP FOUR Remove your hand from the filter and breathe normally. Then get to safety as quickly as possible—the gas mask's canister has a limited filtering capacity, and the clock is ticking.

KNOW THE NUMBERS
Pandemic

200 to 500 million Most people killed by a single disease, smallpox, throughout history.

100 million Most people killed in a single outbreak of a disease, the flu pandemic of 1918.

95 percent Highest mortality rate in a pandemic outbreak—the pneumonic plague of the 1890s.

33.3 million Number of people worldwide who are infected with HIV.

150 million Estimated death toll from a feared H5N1 flu pandemic.

2 percent Odds a new tuberculosis infection will be drug resistant.

2 weeks Time it would take for an airborne virus to spread throughout the world's entire population.

095 Prevent the Spread of Illness

There's a reason why your mother always insisted that you wash your hands regularly, and why public restrooms post earnest signs encouraging the practice. It really is no joke, as proper hygiene can prevent many fatal diseases—you do want to do your part in staving off the next plague, right? In case you need a refresher course, here's how to clean up.

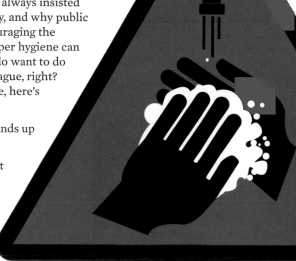

GET WET Start by soaking your hands up to mid-forearm with warm water.

LATHER UP Soap is your friend: It works best to kill organic matter. Rub it in your hands to create a generous lather, and then wash the palms and the backs of your hands, as well as between your fingers and under fingernails. Scrub vigorously.

KEEP TIME Make sure you wash your hands for a minimum of 20 seconds. Longer, though, won't hurt. So whistle a favorite tune while you scrub your hands and wrists, then rinse completely.

DRY OFF Make sure to use a clean, fresh towel after washing. After all that time getting clean, you don't want to contaminate yourself with a dirty towel, do you? I didn't think so.

096 STEP-BY-STEP
Dispose of a Body

If there's a pandemic going on, that means there are dead people. And if infrastructure is down and out, it's up to civilians to take care of the deceased and prevent the spread of infectious disease.

STEP ONE First and foremost, protect yourself while handling the victim. Wear latex gloves, full-body coverage, and a respirator.

STEP TWO Wrap the body in plastic sheeting to keep the remains from contacting anything.

STEP THREE Skip the funeral— otherwise you're exposing other folks to the disease. Bury or cremate the remains as soon as possible.

STEP FOUR Use chlorine bleach to clean anything that might have come into contact with the victim. Burn all clothing and bedding, or put those items in a plastic garbage sack for burial.

STEP FIVE Disinfect yourself and burn your clothing after handling the deceased person.

097 Bunk Up in a Bunker

Remember the Cold War, when the threat of nuclear bombs loomed large and we all readied bunkers in our backyards? Well, contrary to popular belief, that war never ended. Every day countries add to their arsenal of nuclear arms. So if you didn't build that bunker then, build it now. Here's how.

PILE IT ON The goal is to protect against radiation's rays, so the more mass, the better. Construct the roof of steel, concrete, rock, soil, and wood layers, and build your bunker at least 3 feet (1 m) underground.

TRICK IT OUT You're going to be down there for a while; an optimistic estimate is about ten days. That means you'll need several amenities, such as a chemical toilet (which deodorizes waste) and a septic tank, an air pump and a filter, a periscope, and a Geiger counter, which will help you monitor radiation levels.

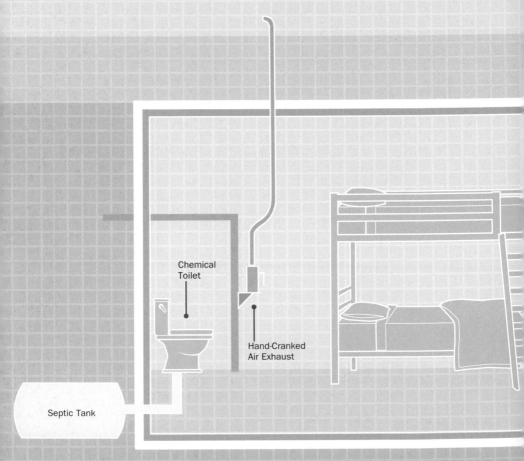

Chemical Toilet

Hand-Cranked Air Exhaust

Septic Tank

STOCK IT UP You'll need food, water, and medical and hygiene supplies for all the occupants, plus clothing and bedding. All in all, figure on 1 gallon (3.75 l) of water per day per person, and gather canned and dehydrated foods (just remember, you need water to hydrate them). Keep a radio and extra batteries so you can keep up with what's going on aboveground, and bring a few books and games to fend off boredom.

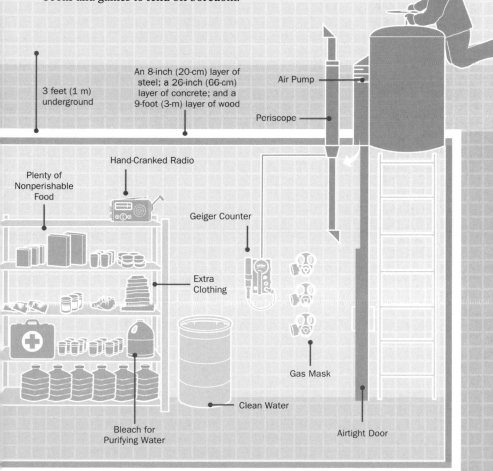

3 feet (1 m) underground

An 8-inch (20-cm) layer of steel; a 26-inch (66-cm) layer of concrete; and a 9-foot (3-m) layer of wood

Air Pump

Periscope

Hand-Cranked Radio

Plenty of Nonperishable Food

Geiger Counter

Extra Clothing

Gas Mask

Clean Water

Bleach for Purifying Water

Airtight Door

098

Anticipate Radiation's Effects

A onetime exposure to radiation is bad enough, but to make matters worse, this stuff can really stick around, lasting from 8 days to more than a billion years. So if a radioactive event happens near you, know that you could be at risk long after the news coverage stops.

WATCH WHAT YOU EAT Animals are the most sensitive to exposure, and guess what: You're an animal. Chances are, you also eat animals and their products—such as beef, milk, and eggs. And many of those creatures eat grasses, which radioactive particles may coat. Avoid eating locally cultivated animal products following a nuclear event, especially if your government issues warnings. You may wish to stock up on potassium iodide tablets, which may prevent thyroid damage. It's best to purchase them prior to an emergency, as demand will quickly outstrip supply.

CONSIDER THE WATER Immediately after a nuclear event, authorities will be testing the local waters to see if they're safe to drink or bathe in, and if fish and seafood is okay to eat. This is when that emergency water stock I've been talking about comes in handy. Use it until you hear that the coast is clear.

THINK BEFORE YOU STAY Depending on the amount of exposure, land that has been impacted by radioactive fallout can suffer long-term damage, rendering it unusable for agriculture or residence for decades. Just because there's no radioactive material spewing into the atmosphere at the moment doesn't mean that it's safe to plant crops, raise livestock, or live in the area. Take, for instance, the land surrounding Chernobyl: It's still uninhabitable, more than twenty-five years after the nuclear accident.

099 Get Through a Power Outage

When the lights go out, it's a sure sign the electrons have gone on strike. You never know how long a power outage is going to last, so it's wise to break out the pack of cards and prepare yourself for a long one just in case.

GO OFF-GRID Turn off or unplug all unnecessary or sensitive electrical equipment (electric stove, computers, TV, sound systems) so an electrical surge or spike won't damage them when the power is restored.

BE REACHABLE Keep an old-school corded phone on hand; it's likely to work even during a power outage.

DEAL WITH LIGHTS Leave one light switched on so you'll know when the power comes back on. If it's nighttime, provide illumination with flashlights and candles.

GO THE EXTRA MILE If someone requires electric-powered life support, provide a backup power supply in your emergency-preparedness plan.

100 Survive a Heat Wave

High temperatures can be more than insufferable: They can be deadly. Worse, everyone using their air conditioners at once can trigger a power outage. If you thought a heat wave wasn't fun, try it without air conditioning. Here's what to do when the mercury rises.

BE SUN SAVVY Open windows on the shaded side of the house. On the sunny side of the house, hang exterior shades to block sun from hitting windows.

PROMOTE CIRCULATION Open the doors and set battery-operated box fans in each entry. They'll expel hot air while drawing cooler air inside.

STAY LOW Remember the old adage about hot air rising? Now's the time that tip comes in handy. Keep to your home's lowest level, where the air is coolest.

GET WET Soak your feet in a basin of water, and wear a damp bandanna around your head. If you have one, fill a spray bottle with water and give yourself a cooling spritz every so often.

DRINK UP Make sure you're getting lots of water, and slow down to avoid overheating. Avoid caffeine or alcohol; they'll only dehydrate you.

UNPLUG IT Your household appliances create heat. Unplug computers and lamps with incandescent bulbs, and make meals that don't require heat-generating appliances, such as stoves.

WATCH FOR WARNING SIGNS Know the symptoms of various heat-related illnesses (such as heatstroke and heat exhaustion). Call the authorities if a someone displays these signs.

101 Eat Right in a Blackout

A power outage suddenly reduces your stovetop to mere counter space and makes your refrigerator no better for food storage than a pantry. But you've still got to eat.

MIND THE EXPIRATION DATE
Open the refrigerator door only when necessary to keep perishables and frozen food fresh. Usually food in the fridge is edible for a day, and food in the freezer for a couple of days.

IMPROVISE A FRIDGE If it looks as if the power outage is going to last a few days or (gulp) a few weeks, you can store your perishable foods in camp coolers or on blocks of ice in the bathtub.

COOK SAFELY A barbecue or hibachi or open fire in the house is a source

of carbon monoxide and a fire hazard. Cook outdoors instead, using a propane grill or Dutch oven and briquettes. If your fireplace has an iron-top inset, you can also cook on that.

APPLY THE SNIFF TEST Discard unsafe foods that have a foul odor, color, or texture. Even when you're hungry, fuzz growing on the food is a bad sign.

102 Start Your Car with a Screwdriver

If you've ever been stranded in dire straits without your keys, you've probably contemplated hotwiring your car. But if your car was manufactured before the mid-90s, you can give the screwdriver trick a try.

Take a flathead screwdriver and cram it into the ignition. It sure ain't elegant, but with any luck, you'll be able to use the screwdriver to turn the ignition cylinder as if you were using your key. Don't worry too much about damaging the cylinder. If you're in a position where you're jacking your own car, damage is the least of your concerns.

103 Siphon Fuel

Siphoning sucks. But sometimes it's your only option.

SET UP YOUR SIPHON Uncap the gas tank and insert a clear, small-diameter tube that's long enough to reach down to the bottom of the gas tank with enough length left over to reach as far as the ground.

START SUCKING Apply suction to the tube with your mouth. Go easy and don't inhale the fumes. The clear tube (hopefully) lets you see the fuel before you get a mouthful.

GATHER THE GOODS Stop sucking when the fuel has reached your mouth (spit out any inadvertent sips you may have taken), then put the end of the tube into a container that's below the level of the vehicle fuel tank. Gravity will do the rest.

104

STEP-BY-STEP
Charge Your Phone with a Flashlight

Crank it up! In survival situations, crank-charging versions of small electronics are mighty handy (literally). Some flashlights and radios work for hours once you've cranked them into full power. Even cooler, you can convert them into basic generators capable of charging a phone or other small device.

STEP ONE Open the housing of the flashlight and locate the package of button cells, which look like a cylinder.

STEP TWO To charge an external object like a cell phone, cut off the plug end of

the charger cord and strip enough of the insulation from the two wires to solder to the corresponding contacts on the button cells.

STEP THREE Turn the flashlight crank to generate power and divert it to your mobile phone.

105
Harness a Car Battery's Power

In survival situations, car batteries can be a godsend. They hold a large charge, and you can recharge them if you have a method for generating current, such as a solar panel. Once you've got it charged, what you do with the car battery is up to you. Here are some ideas.

START A FIRE Mix a small amount of gasoline with tinder and let it rest for a few seconds so the gas fumes can blend with the air above the tinder. Then attach jumper cables to the battery's terminals and strike the positive and negative leads together over the tinder. You'll be rewarded with a spark, and the fumes should ignite immediately.

TURN MASTER WELDER For longer-term use, you can use car batteries to weld. For simple electric welds, connect three car batteries in a series (meaning a connection between positive and negative

terminals) with jumper cables. Connect your ground cable to the first battery's positive terminal and the object to weld. Connect your final cable, with a small wire or rod clamped in the opposite end, to the last battery's negative terminal. As you touch the rod to the object you're welding, the three batteries provide 36 volts and plenty of amperage to perform most basic welds. You'll drain your batteries quickly, so have your weld well planned out before you start.

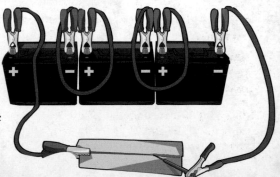

INDEX

A – B – C

abandoning ship 88
aftershocks 52
air travel 83-86
arm injuries 9, 14
avalanches 63-69
blackouts 99-101
bleeding 4
blizzards 70-76
blood loss 8
boating problems 58
BOB (break-out bags) 1–3
body disposal 96
break-out bags (BOB) 1–3
broken bones 9-11, 14
buried by rubble 53
buried in avalanche 67-69
canyon survival 35
car battery, uses 105
car, driving strategies
    in blizzards 71-72
    for car on train tracks 81
    in earthquakes 52
    in fires 41
    in floods 33
    in sandstorms 78
    when stuck in mud 34
car emergencies

no keys 102
out of fuel 103
car survival kit 3
carbon monoxide poisoning
    75
case studies
    firestorm 44
    hurricane 29
cell phones 83, 104
Charest, Armand 29
chemical spills 92
Chernobyl 98
CPR 12, 39
crash sites 86
cruise ship disasters 87-89

D – E – F – G

decontamination 91
disaster preparedness 17
disaster statistics. *See* know
    the numbers
downed power lines 28
downed trees 23
earthquakes 48-55
fallout shelters 97
fault lines 50
fires
    wildfires 41-44

firestorms 44
first-aid
    for arm injuries 9, 14
    for bleeding 4
    for broken bones 9-11, 14
    for burns 15
    for choking 13
    for no breath (CPR) 12
    for no pulse (CPR) 12
    for shock 16
    for wounds 5, 7, 8
first-aid kit 6
flash floods 35-36
flashlights 104
floods 24, 26-27, 29-37
food safety 98, 101
gas masks 94

H – I – J – K

hazardous materials (hazmat)
    90-94
heat waves 100
Heimlich Maneuver 13
help, how to signal
    to air traffic control 84
    from airplane 83-84
    in car in blizzard 71
    from crash site 86

when buried by rubble 53
hurricanes 25-27, 29-31
jumping from plane 85
jumping from train 82
know the numbers
   air travel 83
   disasters 17
   mudslides 62
   pandemic 94
   tornadoes 20

L – M – N

landslides 57
lava 47
life rafts 30-31
lightning 38-40
Lloyd, Jacqueline 44
matches, waterproofing 24
mudslides 60-62
navigation
   in floods 32-33
nuclear disasters 97-98

O – P – Q – R

pandemics 94-96
parachuting 85
plague. *See* pandemics

plane travel 83-86
power outages 99-101
office survival kit 2
radiation 98
rafts 30-31
rescue signals. *See* help, how
   to signal

S – T – U

sandbags 26-27
sandstorms 77-78
screwdrivers 102
ship disasters 87-89
signal mirror 86
slings 9, 14
snowed-in. *See* blizzards
statistics. *See* know the
numbers
stopping a train 80
storms 17-40
stuck in mud 34
survival case studies. *See* case
studies
survival kits 1–3, 6
survival stories. *See* This
Happened to Me
swimming
   away from ship 88

through burning oil 89
This Happened to Me
   panic in the air 86
   tsunami race 56
tornadoes 18-20
train disasters 79-82
tsunamis 56-59

V – W – X – Y – Z

Volcano eruptions 45-47
water, drinkable
   at home 73, 97-98
waterproof matches 24
welding, using car batteries
   105
whiteouts 70
wildfires 41-44
windstorms 21-23, 28
wounds 5, 7

About Rich Johnson

When it comes to survival, Rich Johnson has decades of experience. In the military, he was a paratrooper and demolition sergeant for the US Army Special Forces. In civilian life, he served as a Coast Guard Auxiliary instructor, and was an EMT and a firefighter for a volunteer fire and ambulance department. In his off-hours, he has excelled as a sailor, an advanced scuba diver, and a backcountry skier. He specializes in urban survival skills, emergency preparedness, and primitive living techniques, and spent a year surviving in the desert wilderness with his wife and small children—part of which involved living in a cave and eating bugs (or anything else that moved). He's written extensively on survival topics for *Outdoor Life,* and is the author of *The Ultimate Survival Manual* and *Rich Johnson's Guide to Wilderness Survival.*

About *Outdoor Life*

Since it was founded in 1898, *Outdoor Life* magazine has provided survival tips, wilderness skills, gear reports, and other essential information for hands-on outdoor enthusiasts. Each issue delivers the best advice to nearly 1 million outdoorsmen. And with the recent launch of its survival-themed Web site, disaster preparedness and urban skills are now also covered in depth.

Credits

Cover images Front: *Shutterstock* (first-aid kit, background texture)
Back: *Shutterstock* (photo), *Liberum Donum* (left), *Hayden Foell* (center), *Conor Buckley* (right)

Photography courtesy of *Shutterstock Images* except where otherwise noted:
Alamy: 60
Back Country Access: 69
iStock: 28, 35, 83, 101

Illustrations by *Conor Buckley:* 21, 49-51, 54, 88, 94
Hayden Foell: 10-11, 31, 97
Joshua Kemble: 9, 12, 13
Raymond Larrett: 32
Liberum Donum: Back cover, 26, 41, Tsunami Race, 66, 68, Panic in the Air

William Mack: icons unless otherwise noted
Paula Rogers: 103
Shutterstock Images: 50 (map), 95
Lauren Towner: 105
Gabhor Utomo: 25

Acknowledgments

Weldon Owen would like to thank Marisa Solis for editorial assistance.

All of the material in this book was originally published in *The Ultimate Survival Manual,* by Rich Johnson and the editors of *Outdoor Life.* The original design for that book, adapted here, was by William Mack. Editorial development for the first book courtesy of Lucie Parker and Robert F. James.

Disclaimer

The information in this book is presented for an adult audience and for a reader's entertainment value only. While every piece of advice in this book has been fact-checked and where possible field-tested, much of this information is speculative and highly situation-dependent. The publisher and author assume no responsibility for any errors or omissions and make no warranty, express or implied, that the information included in this book is appropriate for every individual, situation, or purpose. Before attempting any activity outlined in these pages, make sure you are aware of your own limitations and have adequately researched all applicable risks. This book is not intended to replace professional advice from experts in survival, combat techniques, weapons handling, disaster preparedness, or any other field. Always be sure to follow all manufacturers' instructions when using any and all equipment featured in this book. If your equipment's manufacturer does not recommend use of the equipment in the fashion depicted in these pages, you should comply with the manufacturer's recommendations.

You assume the risk and responsibility for all of your actions, and the publisher and author will not be held responsible for any loss or damage of any sort—whether consequential, incidental, special, or otherwise—that may result from the information presented here.

OUTDOOR LIFE

VP, Group Publisher Eric Zinczenko
Editorial Director Anthony Licata
Senior Editor John Taranto
Photo Editor Justin Appenzeller

2 Park Avenue
New York, NY 10016
www.outdoorlife.com

weldon**owen**

President, CEO Terry Newell
VP, Publisher Roger Shaw
Executive Editor Mariah Bear
Editorial Assistant Ian Cannon
Creative Director Kelly Booth
Art Director Diane Murray
Designer Michel Gadwa
Illustration Coordinator Conor Buckley
Production Director Chris Hemesath
Production Manager Michelle Duggan

Outdoor Life and Weldon Owen are divisions of
BONNIER

Library of Congress Control Number on file with
the publisher.

ISBN 13: 978-1-61628-484-8
ISBN 10: 1-61628-484-6

10 9 8 7 6 5 4 3 2 1
2012 2013 2014 2015

Printed in China by 1010 Printing International